Thirty-six million people in this country are suffering from a disease they do not have. They are the families and employers of alcoholics.

Now, there is a book that can really help . . . a book that explains the problems of wives or husbands of alcoholics . . . a book that tells how the alcoholic views the world and how the world views him . . . that tells what practical things must be done to bring the alcoholic to treatment and recovery.

"Her hard-hitting, no-nonsense advice on the pre-treatment phase of this disease should be immensely helpful to concerned families and friends."

—*Publishers Weekly*

RUTH MAXWELL is a former counselor at the Smithers Alcoholism Rehabilitation Center of Roosevelt Hospital in New York City. Currently she is Director of the Occupational Health Services Division of Elden-Maxwell Associates, devoting her skills to helping business and industry establish and implement alcoholism programs.

THE BOOZE BATTLE

Ruth Maxwell

BALLANTINE BOOKS • NEW YORK

Library of Congress Catalog Card Number: 75-36859

ISBN 0-345-28347-3

This edition published by arrangement with Praeger Publishers, Inc.

Manufactured in the United States of America

First Ballantine Books Edition: June 1977
Fourth Printing: August 1979

For Judy, Rachel, and Dan

CONTENTS

ACKNOWLEDGMENTS

I am deeply indebted to my good friend and colleague Robert de Veer, who heads the Smithers Alcoholism Rehabilitation Center of Roosevelt Hospital. Not only was he a constant source of encouragement, but much of what I have said has come from him. I am equally indebted to Rod Elden, president of Rodney Elden Associates, who sponsored *The Booze Battle*. Without the expert services of his staff, particularly Marilyn Trice and Kathy Bradley, his research techniques so freely taught, and his ideas and enthusiasm, the book would be but a dream.

There are many others, but I am especially indebted to Ross Von Wiegand, director of Labor-Management Services at the National Council on Alcoholism, Adolf "Sully" Sullivan, coordinator of Special Health Services, Standard Oil Company of California, and John Williams, director of Special Health Services, Morgan Guaranty Trust Company, for their assistance in the chapter for employers. Special gratitude is also due the Reverend Joseph Kellerman, executive director of the Charlotte, North Carolina, Council on Alcoholism. Not only did he devote many hours to the entire manuscript, but my thoughts in the final two chapters for families were inspired in part by two of his pamphlets, *The*

Merry-Go-Round Named Denial and *AA—A Family Affair*. Vernon Johnson, director of the Johnson Institute in Minneapolis, and the author of the book *I'll Quit Tomorrow*, was also most helpful, especially with the chapter on intervention. Dr. Frank Seixas, medical director of the National Council on Alcoholism, edited the entire manuscript, paying particular attention to the medical data.

The publications of the following were helpful as well: Dr. Richard Heilman's pamphlet, *Early Recognition of Alcoholism & Other Drug Dependence;* Edmond Habib Lahage's pamphlet, *Precipitating a Family Crisis in Alcoholism;* Joan Jackson's paper in the Rutgers December 1954 *Quarterly Journal of Studies on Alcohol,* "The Adjustment of the Family to the Crisis of Alcoholism"; Nada J. Estes' article in the July 1974 *American Journal of Nursing,* "Counseling the Wife of an Alcoholic Spouse"; and Betty Reddy's pamphlet, *Alcoholism: A Family Illness.* Although I have borrowed ideas from far and wide, the concept of a direct public presentation and the words are mine, and because they are, they do not necessarily reflect the views of those from whom I have borrowed.

There would be no book without all the alcoholics and their families who have shared moments of their lives with me at the Smithers Alcoholism Treatment and Training Center of Roosevelt Hospital. I am most grateful to them, as well as to R. Brinkley Smithers, for making that possible. And there would be no book without the incentive and enthusiasm of my children, Judy, Rachel, and Dan, who also assumed the task of renaming the persons whose stories I have presented.

THE BOOZE
BATTLE

There must be something the matter with him
because he would not be acting as he does
unless there was
therefore he is acting the way he is
because there is something the matter with him

He does not think there is anything the matter
with him because
one of the things that is
the matter with him
is that he does not think there is anything
the matter with him

Therefore

We have to help him realize that
the fact that he does not think there is
anything
the matter with him
is one of the things that is
the matter with him.

R. D. Laing

ME SICK?

Soon after I began counseling alcoholics and their families in an alcoholic rehabilitation center, I realized that although there is a great deal of literature available to professionals in the field of alcoholism, very little is available to the people who live or work with alcoholics. The professionals know what should be done, but the people responsible for the doing are left in the dark. Time after time I heard the words "But I have read everything I could get my hands on and I still didn't realize . . ." and "If only I could have known years ago . . ." Believing at first that what I was hearing from these people involved with alcoholics had more to do with their own denial processes than with reality, I nevertheless scoured the bookstores and libraries. They were right. Many books have been written on alcoholism which are available to the public, but none meets the need these people have for specific guidance in the pretreatment phase of alcoholism—the most important phase of all. The people most in need of specific information were actually the people with access to the least. This book addressed to families, friends, and employers of alcoholics is my attempt to correct this tragic situation.

Before I go farther, I will interrupt the train of thought to tell you about a problem I have encountered and try to resolve it so we do not have to deal with it throughout the rest of the book. I have not known what to do with genders. There is no way I can say he (she) and vice versa. We will be hiccoughing throughout the book, those of us who stick it out. One gender or the other has to be chosen. So the masculine pronouns will be used for the alcoholics, while the feminine pronouns will be used for the wives of alcoholics. This will be done throughout the book except where I speak directly about female alcoholics and husbands of alcoholic wives. I can assure you this is purely a grammatical constraint and has no relationship to the relative proportion of male and female alcoholics among the general population. The genders can almost always be transposed in reading without altering the validity of the statement or example, and I must ask each reader to do the transposing according to need.

The pretreatment phase of alcoholism is crucial because it is the phase that causes the most difficulty for the people involved with alcoholics. It is also the phase when, if the alcoholic is approached constructively, he can be reached earlier in his disease process when his chances for recovery are the greatest. Consequently this book is devoted almost exclusively to the pretreatment phase of alcoholism. I do not discuss in detail the actual treatment of alcoholics: Vernon Johnson covers this topic very well in his book *I'll Quit Tomorrow*. Nor will I discuss the recovery phase of alcoholism. If you start doing things differently during the pretreatment phase, I can assure you, you will be prepared for the alcoholic's recovery. You will, you see, have already entered your own recovery period.

I hear you asking, "Me recover? From what? He's

the one who's drinking. He's sick, not me! After all, I'm the one who's held things together all these years." Right you are, but you have paid a price.

Alcoholism is a rough disease. Without fail it causes the alcoholic to act in ways that hurt, which in turn cause you to react by hurting yourself—unless, of course, you are already receiving help. The destruction is subtle in the beginning and always insidious, ever occurring. Most likely you will not realize what is happening or even that anything is happening to you until the time comes when you find yourself screaming at the kids when you are not even angry with them, or crying a lot, or very nervous, or preparing for drastic action which you do not want to take, or feeling just nothing, day after day.

Are you crazy? No, I do not believe you are. I have only met one spouse of an alcoholic who in any way fitted the mold of what we would generally consider insane. All the others had simply attempted to adjust to the unadjustable. That wreaks havoc in the best of us, and it is this havoc, this destruction, that I will speak of; why and how it comes about, and what it is like. I will also tell you why the alcoholic close to you behaves the way he does, what is taking place within him, and how his unpredictability is so predictable. I will also describe new ways for you to respond to him. Not only will you then be better able to help him, but you can end your own destruction and begin the mending of whatever damage has already occurred. Alcoholism is too big for anyone to deal with alone. Without guidance no one can know how to react constructively, because the natural responses we use in other crises do not work in alcoholism. It is as simple as that. I have never met anyone involved with an alcoholic who has not been traumatized to some degree. On the other hand, some of the healthiest people I have ever met are people once caught in the destruction of alcoholism who have gone on to find new responses to living.

I am writing this book because I believe you are *not*

crazy. I believe in your basic core of health and that if you know what to do, you are apt to do it. Many of you have given me reason for my beliefs. You have allowed yourselves to be receptive to new views and new responses. You are very different people today.

I am writing this book, also, not only to give you information about the disease, knowing that knowledge is power, but to tell you of people who can help you, for there is no need for you to be alone. There are at least 36 million people like you involved with alcoholics in the United States. Thousands of you are seeking help and helping each other right this minute; some are in your own community.

Not only can you get well, or protect your present health, by getting help; your alcoholic can be helped as well. Alcoholism is a highly treatable disease, and alcoholics can be forced to an earlier recognition of their condition than they will reach if left alone. They can be forced to earlier "bottoms," but only by certain people. Alcoholics grant that kind of power to but a few—their families (as well as lovers, sometimes close friends) and employers. Because most alcoholics have families and/or are employed, most alcoholics can be forced into treatment by the leverage these people have against them.

Pressure is required. The nature of the alcoholic's disease is such that he perceives neither his sickness nor his need for help. I will describe not only actions for families but actions for employers as well, all of which put pressure on the alcoholic to perceive reality better. None of these actions is particularly drastic in and of itself; all of them or several of them, however, can have an enormous impact upon the alcoholic. None of them is complicated, although few are easy. All are possible, and all help to strengthen the person performing them while creating the climate and the pressure for change in the alcoholic.

I will tell you about some of the people I have known who have been involved with alcoholism. Their names have been changed, but their experiences are real. Sally is the only atypical person in the book, and she is atypical only because she received guidance before she was even sure of her husband's alcoholism. She did all the right things. She is real, but few people identify with her. Ellen and Ken reacted to their spouses' alcoholism in a lot of self-destructive ways, using natural responses which are more typical for most of us. And you will meet others as well, whom I have selected to write about because they too are not unusual. They describe fairly accurately what takes place in alcoholism. If it seems grim, remember that it need not be.

2

SALLY

Sally was nineteen when she married her high school sweetheart, Tom, who was twenty. She was exceptionally attractive, full of energy, and well liked. Tom made friends easily, was a natural athlete, and, along with Sally, eagerly assumed responsibilities in community and church affairs. After one year in college, Tom went to work for his uncle and, having the gregarious charm of the born salesman, was able to help expand the business. Sally was a secretary for a local law firm and enjoyed it enough to continue on a part-time basis after the birth of their children. There was no reason in those early years for either of them to suspect that anything could go wrong in their lives.

But by the time Sally was twenty-six and the mother of two small children, Tom was a full-blown alcoholic. He did not drink daily, performed well in his work, never drank in the morning, and never even had the shakes. However, he did drink heavily nearly every weekend and occasionally on a week night when out with the boys. He drove while intoxicated and had been involved in at least one accident that Sally knew of. She was beginning to live in dread of Tom's killing himself or others. She pleaded, scolded, and occasionally screamed, but to no avail.

When intoxicated, Tom was often insulting to those he was with, including Sally. She and their friends were on guard when Tom drank, for he was becoming increasingly erratic. More and more often he got drunk when he drank. More and more often he became belligerent when he became drunk. Not only was he no longer pleasant to be with on social occasions, he was actually frightening. Several times he had to be restrained from physically assaulting people who inadvertently crossed him. It was not long before friends no longer invited them out.

Following some of his heavy drinking bouts, Tom would be full of remorse and promises for better conduct and less drinking in the future. Occasionally he would feel sick enough the next morning to promise not to drink at all the next time. Sally accepted his promises eagerly and suffered pangs of guilt thinking she had overreacted and should not have said all those things to him. They would make up and Tom would improve for a while, but eventually he always returned to his pattern of excessive drinking and inappropriate behavior.

At work one morning Sally burst into tears. She could no longer contain her despair, her fear, her anger. She felt that Tom's drinking was destroying her marriage and her sense of well-being, yet Tom was not effectively altering the pattern of his drinking. Things were just getting worse. She blurted the whole story out to her boss, who told her then that he was a recovered alcoholic. He suggested the possibility of Tom's being an alcoholic and invited Sally to attend an Alcoholics Anonymous meeting with him.

That meeting was a turning point in Sally's life. Although she couldn't really believe that Tom was an alcoholic, she heard enough to make her wonder. Sally's boss was extremely patient and understanding. He stressed her need for information so she could determine what she was up against. He encouraged her to continue going to AA meetings and to keep an open mind. He also suggested that she go to Al-Anon, which is for families of alcoholics. He said that if Tom was an alcoholic then Sally would be in need of sustained help, both to maintain her own emotional health and to learn the best approaches to the disease. She attended meeting after meeting of AA and Al-Anon and gradually reached some understanding of the disease.

It was helpful for Sally to learn about the loss of control which is the hallmark of alcoholism. She learned that it did not matter how much Tom drank—or when or what. What *did* matter was whether he had control of his drinking or not. Although Sally could see that Tom was very different from most of the people she heard speak at AA meetings, she could also see that these people were very different from one another. Some had drunk around the clock; others had not. Some had suffered physical complications; others had not. Some had hit skid row; others had never lost a job. While some had drunk for years before problems arose, others had had very rapid progressions. Some had been nasty drinkers, others friendly. Some were fat, some skinny. Some rich, some poor. Some educated, some not. No two people seemed alike in any way except for one thing they all shared: a loss of control over their drinking.

Although it was difficult for Sally to accept, she finally acknowledged that Tom, too, had lost his control. She knew he was unable to always predict when he was going to drink, or where or how much. He did not drink during the day or every evening, but he was unable to consistently predict how much he was going to drink when he did drink. Time after time he promised he would have only one or two, yet ended up having his usual amount or more. Occasionally he promised he would not drink at all at a particular event, yet drank anyway. And Tom could not always control his behav-

ior once he started drinking. Although there were lulls
in his drinking and the resulting asocial behavior, he
could not maintain them or stay stopped. Eventually all
his promises and good intentions went by the wayside as
he drank when he intended not to, drank more than he
intended to, or did things while drinking that he did not
intend. Tom was hooked and Sally realized it. He was
an alcoholic!

The moment Sally accepted that fact, she accepted as
well that it was all beyond Tom. Compared to the force
of his addiction he was a dwarf. She no longer believed
that Tom could cut down or stop if only he wanted to,
if only he loved her enough, if only he tried harder. She
knew he needed help.

With her knowledge, her hope, and the help she received from recovered alcoholics and their mates, Sally
set upon a course of action that not only got Tom to the
treatment he needed, but, just as important, a course
that allowed her to cope effectively during a demanding
and painful period of her life. She grew as a person. She
did not succumb to the circumstances surrounding her
because she stopped involving herself in self-defeating
actions. Sally now knew that alcoholism is a treatable
disease. Her employer was an alcoholic, yet alcohol no
longer interfered with his life. She had met scores of
alcoholics in AA who, with the help they received, were
able to stop drinking. She had every hope that Tom too
could be treated.

Sally was one in a million. Instead of falling into a
pattern of destructive responses to her husband's drinking, she took constructive action almost from the beginning, and she was able to do it because she had help.

Sally had revealed her problems to a knowledgeable
person early in the progression of Tom's disease. Her
boss was able to give her constructive assistance and
lead her to sources of information and help. She was
fortunate to have selected a knowledgeable person, because more often than not the people selected as confi-
dants are not informed and cannot give the help so des-

perately needed. Even more frequently there is a reluctance to discuss the problem at all until several years of ever deepening destruction occurs. One recent study indicates that wives wait about *seven years* from the time they first become aware of the alcohol problem to the first time they seek outside help. By then the marriage, if it still exists, can be beyond repair and all the family members so severely traumatized that treatment may not be effective.

Sally was unique on another count. She decided she was not going to wait for Tom to realize he needed help. She feared that if she waited for Tom to have any spontaneous insight of his own, she was in for a long wait. She decided to intervene in the progression of his disease by letting Tom experience his own sickness every way she could.

She had become intrigued with the concept of *hitting bottom*, which she heard mentioned so often in AA and Al-Anon. People reached their bottom, then reached for help. Sally wanted desperately for Tom to reach his bottom, but everyone's bottom seemed to be different and it also appeared to be a mental state rather than a physical condition or set of circumstances. Sally once heard it called *that moment of truth* the alcoholic reaches from a pit of utter despair, when he perceives clearly the futility of his position, the futility of his very being. With that moment of truth the alcoholic will reach out for help if he has hope that help exists and that he is worthy of help. Those without hope are apt to kill themselves. That's how clearly they see their futility and how acutely they feel their despair. This explanation clicked with Sally because it fitted so well with everything else she was hearing in AA and Al-Anon. Sally knew Tom had to feel the pain of despair and futility. She loved him dearly but she knew he would have to perceive his sickness before he would pursue treatment. She was determined to allow him to feel the pain caused by his drinking. She could then offer the hope and help she knew existed.

Meanwhile, Tom did not admit that he even had a problem. But Sally was prepared for this because she heard over and over in AA about the alcoholic's unique ability to deny. She knew that alcoholics could fall flat on their faces, pick themselves up, and claim they had never fallen. What drinking and resulting behavior Tom would admit to he blamed on others: "those nuts she was hanging around with at her meetings," his uncle, her mother, the kids, and anyone else handy. Sally was, as well, hearing ever more frequently that it was her fault. But she did not buy any of this anymore. She knew that blaming outside people and events was but another symptom of the disease.

The alcoholic has to deny, excuse, and accuse in order to continue his drinking. By her attendance at meetings Sally was able to reinforce these facts in her mind. Otherwise she feels she would just have given in, as it would have been so much easier to forget the whole thing and go along with Tom. When he was not belligerent and threatening, he was extremely charming and persuasive. And Tom insisted he had a right to drink; after all, he was working, providing a style of living for his family that allowed for many luxuries, and was entitled to drink when he wished along with all his friends. Sally's response never wavered. She said he had a right to do anything he wished as long as it did not interfere with her life or that of their children. Sally felt acutely that her needs, those of the children, and of the marriage itself were not being met. So much attention was diverted to Tom's drinking—before, during, and after—that the ongoing problems of living were not being coped with effectively. Tom did not have a right to interfere in these vital areas of their lives and none of his protests convinced Sally otherwise.

She stood up for her rights and acted in ways to meet her own needs and those of their children while letting Tom feel his sickness. She refused to compromise because she was determined not to let his alcoholism destroy her, the children, or Tom, if she could help it.

She knew the progressive nature of the disease was such that if it were not arrested everything ultimately would be lost; consequently she was able to take some very courageous actions.

Today Sally and Tom are in their forties. Tom has been sober nearly eighteen years. Both are vital and appealing people and Tom laughs when he recalls Sally's actions. At that time, however, she was driving him right up the wall: "I couldn't come out winning no matter what I did." Sally today says she really did not feel all that strong much of the time. "The only reason I could do it was because of the help I got. My friends in AA and Al-Anon gave me enormous support in many ways but mostly by constantly confirming that what I was doing was right. Much of it seemed so wrong."

What Sally did was to take her focus off Tom's drinking. She no longer extracted promises, knowing they were just going to be broken eventually. She no longer threatened, realizing that Tom did not go by her words. *He listened to action only.* Up until that time her actions had not matched her threatening words. She began to formulate a plan of action that she was prepared to follow through on if Tom refused treatment. She took her attention off his drinking and focused on his inappropriate behavior and need for treatment.

Sally started seeing their friends and family by herself, breaking her own social isolation. She reasoned that because Tom was acting in an unhealthy manner did not mean that she had to, even though she felt awkward at first. She did not look to her friends or family for advice (she knew they didn't have it to give) but calmly stated that Tom had a drinking problem (they all knew it anyway) and that she was taking steps to help him. She carefully stopped her explanations at that point except to add that one way to help him was to remain healthy herself and that she was so grateful they were helping her do this by including her in some of their activities. Sally reports that her friends and family readily accepted her on those terms. Many times she enjoyed herself, although often she would go when she really would have preferred staying at home. Sally forced herself to go because she always felt better about herself for having gone and because her going might allow Tom to compare his abnormal social activities with the more normal behavior of others. She was not only insuring her own emotional health, thereby removing some of Tom's control over her, but was enabling Tom to see some of his own sickness. She could socialize; he could not! *On some level* he was being forced to look at that.

Sally was always aboveboard in her activities, telling Tom about them both in advance and afterwards. Neither her words nor her actions gave him reason to be suspicious. She always made it clear that she wished he were able to join her but the problems related to his drinking made that impossible at the present time. She avoided arguments on this point and remained resolute no matter how angry or contrite or drunk Tom became. After all, Sally reasoned, all he had to do to be with her was to see someone about his drinking problems. Since he was not willing to do that, she was not willing to adjust to the unhealthy social isolation his drinking demanded.

Sally gave up all her attempts to control Tom's drinking. She kept out enough money for the household needs and did not nag Tom about the rest. She hoped the money would not always be squandered on alcohol but was prepared for that to happen and accepted it when it did. Sally also stopped trying to control the alcohol in the house. It was always replaced anyway, and only served to give Tom valid reasons to be angry with her. She no longer hid the liquor or threw it away. In effect, she allowed him to drink any old way he chose, as he had always done even with her struggles and manipulations. She worried about him when he drank away from home, but accepted the fact that she had no control there either. She says, "Many times my prayers were my only comfort."

Sally went further still, taking steps that went directly against everything she had been taught about being a wife and a loving person. She began to let Tom suffer the consequences of his drinking behavior. He had started to become very abusive toward her and on one occasion assaulted her physically. When he could not remember his behavior the next day Sally reviewed it for him, pointing out that such behavior indicated a need for help on his part. When Tom denied both the behavior and the need, Sally told him that if he assaulted her again she would call the police. The next time he started throwing things about the house and it appeared she might be next, she did call the police. When Tom was sober the next day she again reviewed his behavior of the night before for him. Tom remembered the police but flatly refused to speak to anyone about his drinking problem. Sally then said she would have to go to court to get an Order of Protection out against him to protect herself in the future. Tom still refused help and Sally proceeded with her court action. Once again Tom was being offered the opportunity to see that his behavior called for action that does not occur in healthy families.

By providing protection against violence for herself and the children Sally was once again refusing to accept a sick situation as if it were normal. Aside from any physical trauma, Sally had learned at Al-Anon that it would be extremely damaging to her sense of self-worth to allow herself or her children to be physically abused. The positive aspects of calling the police and going to court were far more important to Sally than protecting herself from the shame and embarrassment of seeking such assistance.

Tom's assaultive behavior at home stopped after Sally went to court, but his already excessive drinking increased. He now began to suffer hangovers so severe that he was occasionally unable to go to work. He begged Sally to call his office for him to say that he had the flu and would be in tomorrow. Sally flatly refused to do this under Tom's conditions. She said she knew he was sick and that he needed help: Did he wish it? If he agreed to make an appointment that day with a physician who could help him (she had the name of one knowledgeable about alcoholism) then she would call the office explaining that he was sick and she was taking him to the doctor. Otherwise Tom would be responsible for making his own call.

Sally did not give Tom the angry, silent treatment during these hangovers, but she did not baby him either: she accepted them as inevitable. She simply reinforced her attitude of "Yes, I know you are sick and there is help available." Tom always refused help and Sally allowed him to suffer through his hangovers and to make or not make his own phone calls. Although she was fearful of Tom's job being affected by his drinking, she knew very well that the progression of the disease was such that if he did not get help the job would be lost anyway. Therefore she focused only on Tom's need for treatment, rather than covering for him out of fears of her own.

Sally stopped assuming responsibility for other consequences of Tom's drinking. Whenever his drinking caused him to do things that required picking up the pieces afterwards, Sally allowed Tom to do the picking up, even if the picking up was of Tom himself.

Several times Tom made it home safely after a night's drinking but ran out of steam before making it to bed. Sally let him sleep it off wherever he plopped. She would actually walk over and around him the next morning making her usual amount of noise with the pots and pans and the vacuum cleaner. When Tom came to he would stumble off on his own, but he had to look from whence he picked himself up. *On some level* he was once again being forced to look at where his drinking was taking him.

Sally explained everything she knew about Tom's illness to the children, even though she was not sure they were old enough to understand. She encouraged their normal activities but did not hide Tom's drunken stupors from them. She did shepherd them out of the room when Tom seemed especially aggressive and near violence. At those times she stayed with the children, giving them support at least with her presence.

Once Tom parked his car on his neighbor's front lawn in the middle of the night. When Sally spotted it her immediate temptation was to move it before the whole neighborhood knew. But she asked herself, "Which is most important? Protecting my pride or letting Tom see the result of his drinking?" Sally reasoned correctly that Tom could not perceive the futility of his ways if he did not see his ways. Therefore, when Tom came downstairs at noon, Sally said, "Tom, you parked your car on Ben's front lawn when you came home last night." After an immediate denial from Tom she added, "It's still on Ben's front lawn, and I'm sure he would like you to move it." It's not impossible, but it is more difficult for an alcoholic to deny concrete evidence. Once again Tom had to suffer the consequences of his own behavior.

Sally stopped her efforts to control the environment so life would be easier for Tom. She did not accept his excuses for drinking; that it was the kids' noise, his boss, the neighbors, her mother, or anything she or anyone else did. She knew the problem was within Tom, not in his outside world. Sally reasoned that everyone had problems to cope with but not everyone used alcohol as the method of coping. She stopped all efforts to ease situations in the hope of reducing Tom's need for drinking. She had learned that if she took care of one of his pet annoyances, he would just replace it with another. More than anything he needed his reasons for drinking to continue drinking.

Sally stopped minimizing Tom's behavior. Previously, she had made much of it while he was drinking but little of it when he was sober. Many wives fall into this trap because they are fearful of upsetting the apple cart while peace reigns. Sally correctly assumed that the very time to point out his behavior was when they had a moment of peace. Whenever she attempted to do this when he was drinking she lost her cool, and anyway Tom could not absorb reality and the next day frequently had little or no memory of what had been said the night before. Knowing that Tom always had some guilt and remorse the next day even if he tried not to show it, Sally decided to use it constructively. He would get angry at something sooner or later anyway, and it was important that he become aware of his behavior. She became an expert at nonchalantly reporting the events of the night before. One of her typical reports: "Billy was very disappointed when you didn't show up for his Little League game yesterday. He made a home run and came running over to tell you, but you weren't there. He didn't cry but he wouldn't come down for supper even though I made pizza for him. The manager said it's the first home run he's ever made in a big game."

Now it was Tom who had to live with his own behavior and his guilt, shame, embarrassment, and consequences. He often reacted with anger, but was still being faced over and over again with his own behavior. Sally was no longer as emotionally vulnerable. She still felt hurt very often, especially when the children were involved, but for the most part she was able to recognize his behavior as symptomatic of his disease, thus eliminating a good deal of the pain.

Sally constantly provided opportunities for Tom to see that his behavior was really not normal and that help was available. She removed herself from his drinking and irrational behavior as much as possible. She no longer covered up for him or assumed responsibility for the consequences of his behavior. She no longer tried to control his drinking or his environment. She let him drink, see what he had done, and cover his own tracks, while she went about meeting her needs and responsibilities.

Tom says today, "Nothing was working any more. I was constantly frustrated and I couldn't take it out on

Sally. She just wouldn't be my target." By allowing Tom to make his own bed and sleep in it, she was removing herself from Tom's blame and letting his anxieties increase. Tom was feeling sicker quicker and Sally was accomplishing what she had set out to do.

One particularly bad Monday morning Sally offered to call AA and Tom, for once, agreed. He listened, started going to AA and did stop drinking. However, after a few weeks he reasoned that he was too young to be an alcoholic and had just gone about his drinking the wrong way. He started drinking again and soon became worse than he had ever been. Sally told Tom, in one of his sober moments, that if he wished to drink he must do it from another base; she just did not have the strength to put up with it any more. That afternoon, when Tom left with the obvious intent of drinking, Sally put her plans into action. She installed new locks on the doors, had her Order of Protection ready in case the police had to be called, packed a suitcase for Tom, and left it outside the door. She settled down to wait for his reaction, fearing the worst.

Tom came out of a blackout (temporary amnesia) fumbling with the lock and trying to get his key to work. He says, "Even though I was drunk I knew this was it. I knew she had changed the locks and the ball game was over. Sally always did what she said she would." As he turned to leave he stumbled over his suitcase and any doubts were removed. He was in an absolute panic because he knew there was nothing he could do to change her mind. He picked himself up along with his suitcase and made it to a motel, where he promptly passed out. The next morning he had trouble remembering what had happened, but it slowly came back to him. He knew his only option was to get sober. He was not even sure sobriety would get him back to Sally, but perceived that he needed it anyway. Tom showered and then opened his suitcase. It was packed with dirty underwear. Tom says he just started to cry. "I couldn't even get angry with her. I couldn't blame her any more for anything. It was *me* that got *me* to a strange motel all alone with only dirty underwear, and I knew it." Tom has been sober ever since. He returned to live with Sally and the children when both he and she were comfortable with his sobriety, and then "Our marriage finally began, with all its troubles, all its joys."

3

ELLEN

An alarming phone call from a total stranger with news of her son finally forced Ellen to seek help. There were many things that Ellen had not faced over the years, but one was the gradual retreat of her son into a world of his own. Now she was shocked into action. For several months ten-year-old Steven had been getting on his bike every Saturday and Sunday and riding off for the day. Ellen never knew where he was going, but hoped it was to be with friends—even though she was not sure he had any friends.

On this particular Saturday, Ellen heard that Steven had been riding out to the local airport, where he sat without moving, talking, or apparently seeing. Every Saturday and Sunday he sat and stared from early morning to late afternoon seemingly unaware of either the people or the planes. The stranger on the phone, an employee at the airport, said he often spoke to the boy but never received an answer. Today his concern had mounted when he discovered Steven sitting on his customary bench, unmoving, during a violent thunderstorm. As if in a trance, Steven had followed the employee inside and given, simply, the phone number he was now calling.

Ellen had witnessed Steven's retreat into his own world for a little more than a year. She was aware of his prolonged silences, periodic violent outbursts, poor school grades, and lack of friends, but had not taken action. Now, with the stranger's report on top of everything else, Ellen was desperate. She was facing more than she could handle and more than she could any longer overlook.

The psychiatrist she found for Steven told her the entire family needed treatment. He recognized alcoholism as the problem immediately after talking with Ellen and Steven, and directed both Ellen and her husband, Michael, to the help they each required while he began treating Steven. Michael refused to work with a counselor but Ellen had reached such a point of despair that she was willing to do anything to get help, even if it meant displeasing Michael. She was no longer willing to live the life she had been living, even if it meant that Michael would leave her, which he threatened to do. Ellen today says that it seems as if all their life together she was waiting for the right conditions in order to be happy. "I know now that I was always off in the future. When Steve got so sick, I was finally forced to deal with the present. I couldn't deny it anymore and I couldn't afford to wait for the future."

Her life up until that point had been one of waiting. When she and Michael met and fell in love they were both in college. They could not get married at that time and Ellen envisioned her happiness forthcoming in the future, when they were married. When at last they did marry, Michael was in law school and Ellen was working in a publishing house, patiently awaiting the day when they could afford their own home and children. She had all the dreams: "White picket fences, lots of kids and dogs running around and, me, the supermom."

Ellen had the home soon enough, but eight years passed and several miscarriages occurred before she gave birth to Steven. By that time, although she was overjoyed with the baby and relished motherhood, she harbored a gnawing worry about Michael. His drinking had become a source of contention between them.

On many evenings in the past few years Michael had missed dinner and arrived home drunk. When he was at home for dinner he frequently passed out in the early evening and Ellen had to help him to bed. At social gatherings he became a source of humiliation for her. He was never deliberately rude but he had begun to repeat himself and slur his words; occasionally friends had to help her get Michael home. Twice in the past year he had actually fallen off his chair while eating, once at a wedding and once at a formal dinner party with several of his business associates.

Ellen became a shrew about his behavior. "I nagged him constantly until I finally extracted a promise. He absolutely refused to discuss the episodes and it seemed the only thing I could do was to get a promise for the future." When Michael modified his drinking for certain periods, so that his behavior was socially acceptable, Ellen felt she had exaggerated and was remorseful about her own behavior.

In the first years of their marriage Ellen had not minded Michael's drinking, or if she did, had not complained. She knew his job was very demanding and all the men they knew seemed to drink a lot. Michael was always considerate of her, loved the baby, and had even made their home his hobby. He enjoyed working with his hands and had become a skilled craftsman. To Ellen's delight she did not have to depend on local plumbers and carpenters, for Michael made all the necessary repairs and improvements.

The changes in Michael were gradual, but they were drastic. By the time Steven was four, Michael was having ever more frequent occurrences of inappropriate drinking behavior at social gatherings. He was also taking less interest in the house and their family life and increasingly withdrawing into himself and his alcohol. Ellen says, "He was leaving much of Steve's care and entertainment up to me. He just didn't seem to be interested in anything anymore if drinking was not involved. He had spurts of enthusiasm but rarely followed through."

They started to avoid facing the many problems of living. "When we were making up to each other, I didn't want to talk about the budget, cracked tiles, Steven's lisp, or anything else. And when I was involved in a disturbing situation brought about by his drinking, I was concerned solely with that situation. I was afraid to bring problems in because I felt they would just upset Michael and cause him to drink even more." Ellen and Michael continued to avoid reality for several years to come.

Ellen's concern mounted. Nothing she was doing seemed effective and Michael's drinking was getting worse. She expressed her worries to members of her family and close friends. Several felt that Michael was drinking heavily but most felt she was exaggerating, that it was a rough time in Michael's life and things would get better. Many offered advice for handling specific crises as they arose and it all was conflicting. "I was either to make threats or to be reassuring, to not speak to Michael at all or to talk it all out with him, to ignore him completely or to give him more attention. I just became more confused and felt, somehow, I just had not stumbled on the right approach yet." Ellen's feelings of guilt increased whenever she spoke to anyone. She didn't seem to be helping Michael at all, yet others seemed to feel that if she would do things differently she could help him. She began to feel that perhaps she was actually the cause of Michael's drinking.

When Ellen spoke to the family doctor about Michael's drinking, he agreed to see Michael and to speak to him. He discovered that Michael had an enlarged liver due to alcohol. Michael was told to stop drinking and actually did stop for six months, when a second examination revealed that his liver had returned to normal. Michael was then told he could have an occasional drink, but not to overdo it. Within a very short time, Michael's drinking was right where he had left off six months earlier if not worse. He flatly refused to see the physician again, saying, "He told me I could have an occasional drink and that's all I'm having."

Ellen next spoke to the priest at their church, who suggested a need on both their parts for counseling and recommended a psychiatrist well known for his work with couples involved in alcoholic marriages. Michael adamantly refused. Not only was he angry with Ellen for talking to outsiders, he was also angry at the outsiders for their "meddling" in his affairs. He stopped all his church activities and insisted that Ellen keep her problems to herself. Instead of pursuing counseling for herself, Ellen went along with Michael, who flatly refused to acknowledge any need for any help whatsoever.

Michael also started using her "disloyalty" as another excuse to increase his drinking. By this time anything Ellen did had become reason for his drinking. Even Steven became a reason, and, of course, there was always his job, which had pressures he felt Ellen added to. Without realizing it, Ellen gradually accepted this burden of guilt.

Ellen and Michael gradually entered an almost total social isolation. Ellen is not sure exactly where or how it started, but feels she began to withdraw about the same time that friends and family began to exclude them. "I think I was beginning to see the handwriting on the wall and I wanted to erase it before anyone else saw it. I was scared. I still thought the drinking could be controlled, but I knew there was something very wrong with Michael's drinking. I was ashamed and afraid to have anyone else see the extent of it. I was afraid we'd be ostracized, so I gradually refused invitations and stopped entertaining so people wouldn't know how bad it really was." Ellen also believed Michael when he blamed his upsets on what others said or did, so she withdrew as a way of removing Michael's reasons for drinking as well. "It didn't work and I can see how the isolation hurt us even more."

When there were virtually no other people around them, Ellen and Michael each became even more dependent upon the other's behavior, and they both sank more deeply into the mire of active alcoholism. The isolation reinforced Michael's sense of control over his environment. Now he had only Ellen to contend with and she was becoming increasingly unsure of herself. Michael's need to control his environment was increasing in direct proportion to his loss of control over his drinking. The more he felt the need to drink the more he needed an environment that allowed it.

Because Michael was now almost her only adult contact, Ellen was even more deeply threatened by his inappropriate drinking behavior. She therefore became almost totally preoccupied with Michael's drinking and tried harder and harder to control it. She always failed. When she hid or threw liquor away, Michael became angry and replaced it, or drank away from home. He always had a supply. Ellen threatened to leave him or to lock him out, but she never did, and Michael knew she never would. She babied him, berated him, refused to cook for him, made his favorite dishes, slept in the guest room, slept in his bed with sexy new negligees, ignored him, attended to him solely, wept and laughed. And Michael continued to drink. There was nothing Ellen could find to do that was effective in getting him to modify his drinking, while Michael used everything she did as a reason to drink further.

Ellen was fearful that Michael might lose his job and was terrified at the thought of having anyone in his firm know the extent of the problem. Therefore she never hesitated to cover Michael's tracks any way she could. She was quick to make Michael's excuses for him and on several occasions called his office with detailed descriptions of Michael's "flu" or new case of "intestinal upset."

Ellen also kept Michael from seeing much of his own behavior. She knew that he could not always remember everything from the day or evening before and she did not remind him. She feared that being made aware of either his behavior or memory losses would be upsetting and cause further drinking. She found herself living for those rare moments of peace, hoping each time that then Michael could gain control of his drinking. Consequently she lived from crisis to crisis, soft-pedaling each, vainly waiting and hoping that somehow, someday Michael would be able to get on top of it all.

With every crisis, each found reason to be resentful of the other—Michael because she added to his troubles and didn't understand him, Ellen because she was mistreated and knew it but could not stop it. With each crisis their resentments mounted until that seemed to be the all-pervasive feeling between them. Usually they kept it buried, but occasionally each exploded and when they did, they violently attacked one another both physically and verbally. After a time they accepted physical violence as normal behavior.

Ellen had rages in which she was beyond control: "Once I ran after him with a butcher knife and when I couldn't catch him I just threw it at him. I missed, but only just." She was terrified of her own behavior because she was having feelings and losses of control that she had never dreamed were possible. "I hated myself, but I couldn't stop myself. I would just freak out completely."

It never occurred to Ellen to call the police when Michael, once so considerate of her, became violent. "I would not have done so even if I had thought of it. Police are just not called to settle domestic problems in my town. Besides, I had my own behavior to look at and I was feeling too inadequate to do anything but accept what Michael doled out. What I felt mostly was that I was losing my mind—that I was going crazy."

Ellen spent many years performing actions designed either to control Michael's drinking or to eliminate the reasons for it and every action failed. Each was guaranteed to fail since Ellen never had any more control over Michael's drinking than Michael himself. Each failure eroded Ellen's sense of self-worth. Her self-esteem went down a notch each time until she came to view herself as inadequate, and she became capable of living in a way she would formerly have considered abnormal. She had adjusted to a sick situation and in accepting it as normal came to think of herself as crazy.

Except for short periods when Michael went on the wagon and treated her as he once had, Ellen felt little if any love for him. She had not reached the point of giving up on Michael and feeling predominantly pity—which many wives eventually reach—but she was consumed by feelings of anger, fear, and frustration. She often thought of leaving Michael but never did.

Michael was still working, and in fact his income increased in spite of the extent of his drinking. Ellen had not worked in years and compared her present financial security against slim chances of being able to support herself and take care of Steven alone. Whenever she threatened to leave Michael, Michael threatened to withhold any support from her. He painted vivid pictures of her and Steven living in a cold-water fourth floor walkup. Ellen believed Michael. She had lost all faith in herself. Because she felt guilty for Michael's drinking, Ellen did not feel she had a right to walk out on him, but most of all she feared being alone, so she could not admit failure. "I just would not or could not accept that Michael's drinking was beyond me. We had had so much together at one time and I was sure we could someday return to that. Because he was still working I thought he could also get the rest of his life put together. I really believed that if he loved me enough, if we both tried harder, he could drink normally and then everything would be all right."

Michael's periodic abstinences and occasions of acceptable drinking behavior also kept Ellen from making any kind of stable adjustment. Her hopes and positive feelings for Michael were rekindled each time. Though her hopes were unjustified, they kept her from facing Michael's inability to control his drinking. Instead, she kept trying to pursue the reasons for his drinking and to find ways to control it, all the time feeling more and more a failure as a wife and, in time, as a mother.

Her son got Ellen to the help she so desperately needed. While both Ellen and Michael suffered immeasurable agonies, Steven certainly suffered as much if not more. He changed from an open, alert, affectionate toddler to a ten-year-old so turned in upon himself that several years of psychiatric treatment were necessary before he could cope effectively with his world.

For one thing, Steven did not know how he should behave. He was often rewarded for reasons he could not understand and as often punished for no apparent reason. Steven could not know that his mother was really angry at the father when she struck out against the son, and was therefore guilty and inappropriate in her rewards to him. Nor could he understand his father's withdrawals and silences and then overabundant affections. Steve did not know what to expect or when to expect it, nor did he know what was expected of him.

Steve was raised in a household where inconsistency was his only constant. He knew early that there was something very wrong, but he could not know what. He knew early that his family was different, but not why. His questions were asked but never answered. After all, his parents knew little more than he and were ashamed to speak of what little they did know. Steven knew he could not ask others because "it" was something to be kept secret. It was not long before Steven, turning his feelings of being different into feelings of being ashamed, reduced his own contacts with the outside world.

He felt "it" was his fault, whatever the "it" was. Ellen had herded him to bed "before your father gets home," had requested his silence "so your father won't be upset," and had stifled activities "because Daddy won't like it" so often that Steven grew to believe there was something very wrong with him and he was riddled with guilt.

Steven lived in a cruel world caused and compounded by parents who were not offering healthy modes of coping with life situations. He retreated ever deeper into his own world of fantasies. It was more tolerable there.

The psychiatrist who treated Steven encouraged Ellen to receive counseling at the alcoholism service at their local hospital, even though Michael refused to admit to a drinking problem. Ellen not only learned about the disease, she also learned a great deal about herself and why so much of what she had been doing was destructive—to herself as well as to Steven and Michael. With continued therapy plus Al-Anon meetings, she slowly started the upward path to health. She was able in time to recognize many of her real needs and to assume the responsibility for meeting them. Consequently she was able to bring about new directions to her own life. She did not, however, reach help in time to have any influence in interrupting the progression of Michael's disease. He died before Ellen reached the point where she felt capable of confronting him directly and unequivocally with his needs for treatment.

During the year before his death, when Ellen and Steven were in therapy, Michael's world was rapidly falling apart. His addiction was robbing him of the resources which at one time could have been motivating forces for treatment and recovery. In that year Michael was hospitalized twice with pancreatitis, a condition brought on by alcohol. After each hospitalization Michael stopped drinking for a time but refused to seek any help to stay sober. His doctors suggested AA but Michael still flatly refused to believe he was an alcoholic. He was willing to admit to a drinking problem but refused AA because he did not feel he was as bad as all that. He felt that because he was still working he could not be an alcoholic.

And then he was no longer working. A few weeks after his second hospitalization, Michael lost his job. Ellen later learned that Michael had been warned about his drinking on several occasions and was finally forced to resign when he did not comply with the firm's warnings. His employers, as uninformed about the disease as Ellen, reacted to it as if Michael had control over his drinking. They did not recognize his need for treatment and, consequently, did not use all the power at their disposal to get him to the help he so desperately needed.

After his forced resignation Michael started drinking more heavily than ever. While driving home from a bar, where he had been drinking most of the day and evening, Michael started vomiting large amounts of bright red blood. He was hemorrhaging from ruptured blood vessels which had become enlarged in his throat, a condition secondary to the liver damage of alcoholism. He was found in a pool of blood in his car alongside the road by an early morning passer-by. He had been dead for hours.

Ellen was not the cause of Michael's alcoholism. She and their child were, in fact, nearly destroyed because of it. But all the destruction and Michael's wasted life were needless. *Alcoholism is a treatable disease!*

4

WIVES OF
ALCOHOLICS

The wife of an actively drinking alcoholic who responds to the disease by herself, without either knowledge or help from knowledgeable people, can only lose. So does her husband and do so her children. Her actions are such that she actually helps her husband to drink. Her actions are such that she herself becomes emotionally unstable and raises emotionally crippled children. She is in desperate need of help, but puts it off until *she* perceives *no other choice*.

There must be something within all of us that allows us to sit back without constructive actions until the moment is at hand when we are finally forced to move. Why else are we suddenly sitting on top of the energy crisis volcano? We have known for years that it was coming. Fifteen years ago I spent a semester studying about the impending ravages of the population explosion. The notes I took at that time outline events that would occur if corrective measures were not taken; shocking events which today are occurring. Is there any-

thing I could have done? I don't know. The point is
that I, along with many, did nothing. Constructive action often brings momentary discomfort which we will
pay almost any price to avoid. Perhaps it is part of
being human to take constructive action only when
there is finally *no other choice*.

As people in general cannot afford to wait, the wife
of an alcoholic especially cannot afford it, for alcoholism is as progressive and clearly predictable as the energy crisis or the population explosion. Effective measures for halting its destruction demand that the wife
rise above herself, above her humanness. A tall order
indeed, yet that is what is asked of her.

As if that alone were not enough, the wife has other
hurdles before her. Traditionally our society has placed
women in a dependent position. Although this is changing today as women redefine themselves, for the most
part the status of the wife is still based on what her husband does and how well he does it. Consequently she
feels in immediate danger if her husband's performance
is in any way adversely effected. Her natural survival
reaction is to make things all right. She urgently feels
the need to control her husband, to manipulate him, to
get his performance back up to snuff and keep it that
way, and to cover poor performances any way she can.
In doing what comes naturally, she provides the ideal
environment for her husband to drink further, ensuring
the very thing she is most fearful of: a worsening of the
situation.

And it does not stop there. The wife is further im-
pelled by old tapes programmed since infancy, which
she has whirling around inside her telling her how to be
a good wife. And that involves, so her tapes tell her,
nurturing, caring for, a little nursing and doctoring now
and then, being kind, sympathetic, understanding, and
responsive to her husband's wishes. She is programmed
to do all this and the better she does it, the better wife
she is. And the sicker her alcoholic husband becomes!

Natural "wifely" responses that a traditional marriage calls for only further the progression of alcoholism.

Constructive approaches to alcoholism require the wife to go beyond herself. She must be willing to forgo her desires for immediate comfort, because to effectively interrupt the progression of alcoholism and its destruction she must face and cope constructively with each crisis as it arises, hoping that something good can come of it but without specific guarantees. Whenever she feels compelled to cover her husband's tracks or to rescue him from a situation out of her own feelings of shame, embarrassment, or fear, she will have to face these feelings and take actions not necessarily designed to reduce or alleviate them. She will have to embark upon new behavior designed instead to interrupt the course of her husband's alcoholism. She must be willing to adopt the all-abiding faith that if she is doing the right things for the right reasons, good will come of it. Exactly *what* that good will be, or *when*, is out of her hands. She must let go of the results and concentrate on the necessary constructive action at hand. To discover her best options and act on them, she will need help.

The wife of an alcoholic must become willing to let go of the idea that she has any control over her husband's drinking. Each time she manipulates or controls in any way, she fails. That's a guarantee. No matter how determined, attractive, clever, knowledgeable, strong, or sly she is, she cannot overcome the force of her addicted husband's need for his fix. A modern-day Cleopatra would not have that much power. The most any wife should hope and strive for is emotional health for herself and treatment for her husband.

Every attempt at controlling either her husband or his environment will backfire, and her husband will gain the further control which he needs in order to continue drinking—to satisfy the compulsion of his addiction. When she feels the urge to control, she will instead have to face her own fear, anger, and anxiety. She will have to substitute constructive actions, for only then does she stand a chance of getting her husband to treatment and of keeping her own emotional health.

She will have to give up for the time being some of her preconceived ideas of what a loving wife is. What her alcoholic husband needs is described by some in the field of alcoholism treatment as "tough love," which requires that she act in ways that go against what she and society conceive her role to be. Her behavior may seem callous to the casual observer but it is based on a love that has the husband's vital interests at heart, a love that grants him the opportunity to feel his own sickness and to get treatment. This is not the kind of love that caters to his expressed wishes and demands, no matter how persuasive or threatening he becomes.

What wife is prepared for these measures? Few are! Few are until they perceive they have *no other choice.* By then it may be too late.

There are some wives who are no longer waiting, who have gone out to seek knowledge and help for themselves so they may better respond to their husband's disease. These women are not counting on Sally's luck in finding the right help by confiding in the first person who comes along. They are seeking out alcoholism services and specialists. Like Sally, however, they are discovering new ways of approaching the disease and are redirecting their lives instead of adjusting themselves to the sick situation of alcoholism.

Unfortunately, Ellen is far more typical. Like her, most women are still waiting years after they are aware of their husband's drinking problem before they reach out for help. Like Ellen, they do not confront the disease early, when there are fewer problems and less trauma. They allow the disease to progress to the point where an outsider looking into their lives would ask, "What could be worse? Why doesn't she do something?" The answer this outsider would get would be, "But I've tried everything and nothing works." In reality she's only tried all the "home remedies" and, true, they don't work. The next question would be, "Why does she put up with it?" The answer, "Because I perceive something even worse." Being alone and on their own is so terrifying to some women that they are willing to put up with what others would consider a shocking existence. No matter what their present pain is, it does not appear to them as horrifying as the circumstances which change might bring about. No price is too high as long as a person is determined to pursue a desire for comfort by escaping projected fantasies of pain. Wives of alcoholics pursue this desire for comfort as if it were a need, when, in fact, facing pain is their need. It is the only way for them to reach healthy resolutions or to obtain the emotional strength to cope with the recurring crises of active alcoholism.

I am not recommending pain for pain's sake, but if it is present it provides an opportunity to build emotional muscle, to acquire greater personal strength and tolerance for life's discomforts. The wife of an alcoholic does not have to look for pain: it is dropped in her lap by the never ending crises caused by her husband's drinking. When stressful situations are met and coped with constructively, the wife gains in her sense of self-worth. She feels stronger and better prepared to deal with further crises in the future. She gains personal power. When she either flees stressful situations or does not cope with them constructively she robs herself of personal power; her feelings of inadequacy increase and she is more poorly prepared for future crises. What the wife does, then, with the crises presented by her husband's drinking will either make or break her.

Ellen ran from the pain of facing her worries about Michael's drinking. When the priest she consulted suggested that Michael might be an alcoholic and recommended counseling for her, Ellen chose instead to listen to the family physician, who recommended simply that Michael cut down. She chose to believe that Michael could cut down rather than face the pain of exploring the possibility that Michael was an alcoholic. She chose a route that was the most comfortable for her at the moment and as a result entered a denial of the disease that complemented Michael's own. Unfortunately, this is the typical pattern. Rather than face the possibility of alcoholism, wives of alcoholics are as inclined as the alcoholics themselves to examine definitions of alcoholism and pick the one that does *not* apply rather than explore the ones that do.

Sally, too, felt pain when her boss suggested that Tom might be an alcoholic. She was very upset and became even more so when she started investigating the disease and could not convince herself that Tom was not an alcoholic. She says she became more anxious every day. "I was so afraid of what I heard at those meetings that I actually got sick. I had such nausea that I couldn't eat on the days I had to go to a meeting. I used to hope the sitter wouldn't show up so I could stay home." She finally felt better when she found out enough to know beyond any doubt that Tom was an alcoholic. When she accepted his disease and no longer struggled to deny it, she felt quite hopeful and at peace with herself for the first time in years. It also gave her new strength: "From then on, every time I faced a situation and handled it well I felt strong enough to handle the next one."

Far too many women become defeated before they start because they opt for action that will bring them immediate comfort rather than action that has a chance of being effective and therefore strengthening to them. Not only do they enable the disease to progress, they become less adequately equipped to cope with it as it worsens. By avoiding pain, they are ensuring their greater pain.

A woman who is married to someone whose drinking is in some way hurting her should ride with her anxiety long enough to find out what she's up against. If her husband is only a heavy drinker and is able to modify his drinking so as to no longer hurt her, then she has gained a lot and lost nothing. Certainly if her husband is not dependent upon alcohol, the chances are he will not object to her quests for knowledge since he will not feel threatened. She can feel proud of herself for demonstrating the willingness to explore any avenue for guidance in strengthening herself and their marriage.

If the quest for information ends with the conclusion that her husband is an alcoholic, she is then in a position to get the help she will need. She will not have to stumble along the destructive route and she will not be alone. With knowledge and help she will be able to take constructive action to maintain her own emotional health. In so doing she may be able to interrupt the progression of her husband's fatal disease.

Virtually every wife who is responding to the disease of alcoholism by herself is guided by two specific principles that set the tone for all her actions and that ultimately guide her toward her own destruction. First, she attempts to control her husband's drinking, and second, she concentrates on his reasons for drinking and attempts to eliminate them.

The fact that her husband cannot control his drinking is the problem, not the solution. This simple fact eludes her for years. She explores virtually every way she can dream up to get him to drink less or not at all. If he had control, there would be no problem and no solution would be necessary. All her attempts to get her husband to control his drinking are futile, since that inability is his very problem. She wastes herself, and precious time, in attempting to instill such control in her husband.

She threatens, but he drinks anyway. She screams, cries, and wheedles promises, yet he continues to drink. She hides the alcohol or throws it away, so he drinks outside the home or brings more in. She becomes tender, loving, and yielding, but although he may enjoy her more, he still drinks. She drinks to become drunk with him, often going on to alcoholism herself, yet he continues to drink. She takes his money, but he borrows or charges. She removes herself physically from her husband—"no sex with booze"—so he chooses the booze. She could stand on her head and spit pennies in an attempt to control her husband's drinking, and he would still drink.

With every attempt at controlling her husband's drinking, the wife creates new sources of anger for her husband to use against her and as reasons for further drinking. He has but another complaint to lay before his favorite psychiatrist, the local bartender. By attempting to control her husband she is setting herself up as a target for his frustrations and is granting him the very justifications for drinking that he is looking for.

Further, with every attempt at control of her husband, and the failure that results from each attempt, the wife comes to feel less and less adequate as a person. She always fails and she thinks of herself as a failure. Soon she feels insecure in every sphere of her life. She becomes more easily manipulated and controlled; she abdicates power to her husband, who increases his control over her. Thus it becomes increasingly easy for him to drink the way he wants to without outside interference. By attempting to control her husband, the wife is actually granting him the dream of every alcoholic: the freedom to drink the way he wishes. In every way it is dangerous for the wife, for her sake and her husband's, to attempt to control his drinking.

A wife will often believe she must control her husband's drinking for his sake—that he will be killed in an accident if he does not stop! True, he might be. Alcoholics are not known to die peacefully of old age; most of them die violent deaths at relatively early ages and most have people around them still vainly trying to instill controls in them. The wife must accept the fact that there are certain things she cannot control, and one of them is her husband's drinking. She must give up and accept the fact that she is not God. Only then can she apply her energies to those things she can change, so that she does not adjust to a sick situation as if it were normal.

Another fact the wife overlooks is that her husband drinks the way he does because he is addicted. He has, for whatever reasons, learned to cope with life through the use and abuse of alcohol. He is trapped in a maladaptive response to living that will kill him unless he is treated. He has developed a psychic dependence which, unless he receives treatment, will go on to a physiological dependence and premature death.

During the active addiction it is virtually impossible to discover the reasons why he chose this way of living in the first place. But, even more important, if the reasons could be discovered he would still be left with the addictive drinking itself. Before an alcoholic can explore and learn new modes for coping he must first give up the chemical one he is using, and for that he requires special treatment.

Wives of alcoholics spend an inordinate amount of time and energy trying to discover the reasons, past and present, for their husbands' drinking. They become preoccupied with events, circumstances, people, places, and things in their husbands' lives. They believe it is forces in this outside world that are somehow causing it all, and, sadly, they often assign themselves first place among these causes. They do not see the addiction that has to be fed at *any* cost, no matter what is or was taking place in the life of the alcoholic.

Any time a wife concerns herself with what might or might not affect her husband's drinking, she is out of touch with the addiction, the only factor which is going to affect his drinking in any way. Whenever a wife tampers with the environment of her husband in an effort to reduce his reasons for drinking, she is treading upon dangerous ground, because the end result will serve only to allow her husband to drink further.

First, because of her concern that the environment remain or become comfortable in order to eliminate reasons for her husband to drink, the wife is forced to withdraw them both from social contact. She believes that other people are upsetting her husband and causing him to drink; after all, he tells her that often enough. She is very fearful that people will say or do something that will set her husband off and running into yet another drinking spree. She therefore manipulates their lives so that normal social contact with family and friends either does not occur at all or does so very tenuously; contacts are nervous and brief. She then hangs on to her husband's not being able to socialize as an excuse to curtail her own involvement with the world, for she believes that if she has contact with others without her husband he will become upset and drink even more. He, of course, will! He *will* become more upset and *will* have another excuse for drinking. What the wife does not realize is that *he will become upset and find an excuse no matter what she does.* She also does not realize that as her social isolation increases, she becomes more dependent upon what her husband does. By increasing the isolation, she is setting up a cycle whereby she keeps losing power to her husband, who keeps gaining further control over his drinking environment.

When the husband is virtually the only contact a wife has, she is increasingly influenced by him. Isolation increases her dependence and she becomes even more eager and willing to grant his requests and respond to his threats. "Maybe then he'll stop!" She willingly, even desperately, makes calls, apologies, excuses, and reparations, hoping everyone, especially the boss, will forgive, not notice, or offer another chance. As her husband gets worse she feels further threatened and increasingly compelled to reduce his reasons to drink. She tries even harder to eliminate all possible reasons within their world for him to drink. This works just as disastrously as throwing his booze away; as soon as one reason is eliminated, he finds another, and his control over her is increased with her every failure. When she amasses enough failures she will begin to question her own sanity.

Second, in an attempt to reduce reasons for drinking

the wife will hide her husband's own behavior from him if she can. She does not want him to suffer the consequences of his drinking because she reasons this would be so upsetting to him that he would then have further justifications to drink. She is quick to pick up the pieces after her husband in order to reduce his need to drink. He has her exactly where he wants her. As he drowns his pains in alcohol, she surrounds him with a blanket of comfortable unreality. Instead of making it increasingly difficult for the husband to accept his own behavior and be that much closer to treatment, she makes his drinking increasingly easy for him to tolerate.

While the wife is busy making changes in her husband's environment to reduce his reasons for drinking, she eliminates his incentive to make the *one* change that is needed, *treatment for his addiction*. As with her attempts at controlling her husband's drinking, her attempts to alter his environment to reduce his reasons to drink serve only to enhance his ability to drink further without interference.

Today thousands of wives are learning how to approach their alcoholic husbands differently. They are stopping the old actions which abetted their husbands' drinking, and which increased their own misery. They are substituting new actions which make it increasingly difficult for their husbands to continue drinking. In the process the wives are regaining their sense of self-worth and their freedom. *They are no longer puppets to their alcoholic husbands, therefore their husbands are forced to change; many are getting sober!*

5

KEN

Ken made up his mind on the 8:37 to New York. He'd leave and take the kids. Barbara could have the house. "She's got her car and I'll send her money for food." He'd done everything he could. "She wasn't even up this morning for Chrissake!" He'd gotten the girls up and given them breakfast. He'd even brushed their hair before sending them to school. "Jesus, she just lies there stinking up the whole room . . . a good lay turned into a reeking, stinking mess!" And now he had to go to Europe. "That's Barbara's fault too. If I didn't have to worry about her and the kids all the time, I wouldn't have made that mistake in the contract in the first place. Now I'll be lucky if I'm able to salvage any profit. . . . Mother will take them. She said she would—at least till I get back."

Ken didn't know where it all started or how. Everyone had wanted Barbara, but she married him. Ken felt lucky and proud. Barbara could do anything and she was always fun to be with. "Jesus, the house is a showplace. She finds these kooky things and turns them into eyestoppers. . . . She's an eyestopper. Two kids and she still fills a bikini better than anyone else. Why the hell is she drinking like this? Why is she so jumpy? . . . God, I wish she'd take care of the kids better."

Ken was afraid and confused. He couldn't figure it out. "She just started drinking a little like the other wives and the next thing you know she's drinking all the time." He didn't remember her drinking much when the kids were little—just before dinner and at parties. "She didn't even get tipsy . . . Christ, she was the one who drove us home . . . and now I never know what she's going to do."

According to Ken, Barbara had reached the point where she was drunk most of the time. Usually she got up before everyone else, but by the time she was getting the girls off to school she was already slurring her words and speaking louder than normal. "And she'd be full of energy and great plans for her day, but the girls would find her asleep and still in her robe in the afternoon when they returned from school." Barbara would drink until she passed out and never did anything until late in the day, at which time she would pull herself together enough to get the marketing done and the house picked up. But it would be a miserable time for Jodi and Suzanne because Barbara would be very pressured and irritable. Anything they did irritated her further and she invariably ended up screaming at them—most particularly at Jodi, who was nine, and whom Barbara found more irritating than Suzanne, who was eight.

By the time Ken arrived home for dinner, the girls were often crying and sometimes even barricaded in their room. They were afraid of Barbara, who would occasionally slap them to get them out of the way. And dinner would be a mess before it even started. Parts of the meal would be burned, parts nearly raw. The girls would be silent, either weepy or sullen with anger, and Barbara would start drinking again and stagger, sashay, slur, and sleep her way through the rest of the evening.

Ken would be beside himself, but he was usually able to control his temper till the girls had done their homework and gone to bed.

He tried everything he could think of. He warned and threatened, but was never heeded for long. He took long walks to keep himself from hitting her. He hid the booze and restricted her money. He hired housekeepers to help with the girls and to relieve her of her household chores, but they never stayed long. Barbara was intolerable; each complained bitterly to Ken about Barbara's demands and incessant criticisms before they stalked angrily off. He took the girls out for dinner in the evenings—sometimes encouraging and helping Barbara pull herself together enough to join them, sometimes without inviting her at all. He found a psychiatrist for her, but after a few sessions Barbara called him stupid and refused to return. He appealed to his family and to hers. One group encouraged divorce, the other group blamed him for causing Barbara to drink, for not understanding her. Neither was able to offer any advice Ken found helpful. Ken didn't want a divorce, he just wanted Barbara to stop drinking and be the way she used to be. He knew he worked hard and kept long hours, often traveling for two or three weeks at a time, but "Christ, I was bringing in the bread. There was nothing I wouldn't give her." Yes, he did have an occasional fling, "but nothing that amounted to anything. Barbara refused to sleep with me or would be so drunk I wouldn't want her. I had to do something or I'd have blown my top. What made her a lush? That's what I can't understand."

Barbara had been an honor student, editor of the college newspaper, and homecoming queen. She was vivacious, pretty, talented, and bright. What went wrong? She had worshiped Ken. She loved his strength and good looks. She knew he was a winner, which he was right from the beginning. She took to their surburban community like a duck takes to water. She kaffeeklatsched, committeed, and chauffered school car pools

along with everyone else. Just last year she had headed
a fund-raising committee that brought in more than
they projected. She did get drunk at one of the lun-
cheons, but only that one time. "And now she's dead.
God, what could I have done? I never should have left
her like that."

Ken returned from his salvaging trip to Europe three
weeks later than he expected. It had taken him six
weeks to get his business in order. Jodi and Suzanne
were with his mother and had adjusted well to their new
school. They seemed more relaxed, but Ken worried
when they said they wanted to stay with their grandmother. Barbara had been making frequent phone calls
to them, always drunk and often threatening and pleading at the same time. The girls seemed even more fright-
ened of Barbara now than they had been before moving
in with their grandmother. Ken's mother also expressed
her worry and anger. She felt strongly that Barbara was
ruining the children and should not be allowed to have
them, and she was more than willing to raise them herself, especially because she still had her large home and
a doting housekeeper to help her. She knew it would be
better if their own mother raised them but Barbara
would have to pull herself together first.

Worried and anxious, Ken drove to his home. The
scene he encountered was worse than anything he could
have imagined. With the girls and Ken away, Barbara
had no longer needed to control herself; she could drink
as often and as much as she pleased. Every light in the
house was on. Furniture was turned over and upside
down, curtains were pulled from the windows, every
mirror was smashed; every dish, cup, and glass had
been bashed into the walls. Porcelain and glass chips
were scattered over everything. The refrigerator door
was open; burned food was on the stove—it looked
weeks old. The heat was turned off and the house temperature was near freezing. Empty vodka bottles were
everywhere. When Ken went upstairs Barbara awoke
from a drunken stupor and fell into his arms. She clung

to him desperately, sobbing convulsively. She was frail—she had lost nearly twenty pounds. He retched at the sight and smell of her. Barbara pleaded with him not to leave her. She promised she would never take another drink as long as she lived if only he'd stay.

Ken stayed and Barbara did stop drinking. A house-cleaning service was hired and the house was put in order; china and dishes were replaced. Barbara soon felt strong enough for the girls to return—that seemed to be the only thing she wanted. Ken says everything was great for a while, or almost great; Barbara was nervous and didn't laugh as readily as she once had, but outside of that everything was good. "I was sure she had it made. She started seeing her friends again and we even had people over for dinner. Barbara served them drinks without touching any herself." Ken never thought she'd start drinking again after the mess she had gotten into, but he was wrong.

Barbara picked up a Bloody Mary at a luncheon with friends and within two weeks she was drinking around the clock. Jodi and Suzanne were pleading to return to their grandmother's and Barbara was vicious with Ken. She maintained that she could stop drinking anytime she wished. The girls could go to their grandmother's—Ken's mother had already ruined them and "She might as well finish the job—that will make her happy." Barbara was sure everyone was against her.

A friend of Ken's had told him about AA, but when he mentioned it to Barbara she flew into a rage and started accusing him of not caring for her. She told him that it was all his fault, he was never home and she was sure he loved another woman. She also called him sick and told him he should see a psychiatrist. She demanded that he leave along with the girls; she would be better off without them, since none of them cared for her anyway. And with that she stormed off, locking herself in her room, refusing to come out until they left the house.

Ken felt it would be best to take the girls to his mother's and then return to appeal to Barbara to stop drinking again. "I had never seen her in a rage like that. I knew I had to protect the girls. I couldn't do anything with them around. They were scared to death.

"When I got back she was drunker than ever and she had put on one of those sexy negligees. She was slinking around like Marilyn Monroe for Chrissakes. And she picked me apart. She told me she had never loved me, that I was lousy in bed and that other men satisfied her but I never had. When I asked her what other men, she told me about her daily affairs with delivery boys, repairmen, and even the mailman. She didn't spare me the details either. Jesus, she even told how she got on the kitchen table and let them do it to her there. I thought I was going to kill her. I fled when I found myself with my hands around her throat. I must have driven all night. I washed up in a gas station and drove to my office. When I got there, Barbara called saying the telephone repairman was on his way and would I like to learn how a man makes love. Jesus, I couldn't go home—not even when she called later in the day to say it was a lie, there had never been any men. I didn't know what to believe, but I felt she was capable of anything."

Barbara telephoned several times, pleading with Ken to return and promising to do anything if only he would. Ken said he would have to think about it. He was not at all sure he wanted to return to Barbara. He certainly didn't want to touch her. He didn't know whether he would ever trust her again. He was deeply hurt and full of anger. Finally he promised to visit over the weekend.

Barbara looked pretty good for the visit but Ken could smell alcohol on her breath. At first she was casual and businesslike. She promised she would stop drinking if he returned and they could then work everything out together. She said it had all been her fault and she loved him very much. She asked him to please forgive her, she hadn't meant any of the things she had said. She wanted another chance; she was willing to do anything he said.

Ken was undecided and, sensing rejection, Barbara reacted quickly. She accused him of not loving her, of never having loved her, of having another woman, and of wanting to take her daughters from her. When he protested, she started attacking him, calling him a mother's boy, a rotten husband and lover, and screaming for him to get out of the house, which he did.

Ken sent her money regularly. On occasions when he accepted her phone calls he said that he would see her only when she had stopped drinking, and that he couldn't promise he would return to live with her even then. Since she always sounded as if she had been drinking, he didn't see her again until he was called to identify the body.

Barbara had run out of booze late one snowy evening. Because the liquor stores were no longer delivering, she was forced to leave the house to get some more. She left with just a raincoat covering her nightgown and only sandals on her feet. No hat, no gloves, no stockings, no boots. She was on her way to her car, parked in front of the house, when she slipped on the ice. The fall did not kill her, but it knocked her unconscious. The freezing temperature killed her. She froze to death in a blanket of snow.

Although Barbara's alcoholic progression was fairly rapid, her story is by no means unique. She desperately needed help, but the personality changes brought about by alcohol, plus Ken's lack of knowledge about the disease, made it impossible for him to get her to treatment. Because he was uninformed he was unable to remove himself emotionally in order to see her needs. Instead he was shocked by her behavior and believed the things she said. He despised her and at the same time yearned for what had once been.

Ken believed that she was deliberately destroying herself and was deliberately trying to destroy him and the girls. He hated her for making him feel cheap. He hated her for not being a good wife and mother. Instead of seeing her behavior as symptomatic of her disease, he believed and was crushed by her words. He felt he had given Barbara everything a woman could ask for. She had complained because he was always working, but "she liked the clothes and the house and everything. I even got her a convertible when they weren't making convertibles. I was working hard for *her*, for Chrissake. Why did she have to ruin it all?"

Ken is only now beginning to get an understanding of the events that changed his life. It will be some time yet before he works through the residue of his anger and his enormous guilt to a point where he can return to his former level of functioning. At present Ken admits that he is afraid of women, that he doesn't want to get close to them and often uses them cruelly in desperate attempts "to feel like a man."

Although Barbara's progression was rapid, it nevertheless seriously traumatized her husband. Jodi and Suzanne are also in therapy. They are having a difficult time thinking of themselves as worthy. They too feel that if they had stayed home and acted differently their mother would still be alive.

Barbara could have received treatment. Several times she reached a point of being willing to do anything to get Ken back—perfect opportunities to offer and insist upon treatment, if only Ken had known how to deal with her disease.

Alcoholism is deadly! It kills and destroys those not prepared to cope with it.

6

HUSBANDS OF ALCOHOLICS

It is manly to drink! Two-fisted male drinkers are our heroes, and have been since before the days of the Wild West. Little boys should grow up and learn how to drink like them. In our society the male drinking myth is so strong it is considered *unmanly* not to drink!

Society's attitude toward female drinkers is somewhat different, in fact it is often the opposite. If a woman must drink, she should drink like a lady. She is not generally required to drink, but she may on occasion, if she has only a little. She may *not* become unladylike with her drinking or she will be considered a lush.

Society says it's O.K. for a man to get sloshed. It's expected occasionally. It's even funny—some of our most popular cartoons are built on just that theme. Not so for women. Society expects them to control themselves—to *not* get sloshed. If they do, it's by no means funny, it's disgusting! Even though the drunken behavior of women differs little from the drunken behavior of men, drunken women are considered disgraceful. They are lowered a considerable number of pegs in the esteem of others as well as themselves. Men can get sloshed without the same lowering of esteem.

The different attitude we have about female drinkers has an enormous effect on our approach to the female alcoholics in our midst. They are not as acceptable as male alcoholics because they have overstepped the boundaries allowed by society for female drinking. Consequently they are not considered deserving of help. Society does not make the same allowance for their alcoholic drinking as it does for men. A recent article in the London *Times* points this out in reporting the results of a random sampling of people's reactions to alcoholics. The most common view of the male alcoholic was, "The poor soul! His wife drove him to it!" and of the female alcoholic, "The poor husband. He deserves better than that!"

Traditionally women have been placed, or have allowed themselves to be placed, in a dependent position in relationship to men. Women, especially wives, are expected to cater to their men and to their men's careers. Their role in traditional marriages calls for them to care for their husbands, their children, and their homes, placing those interests before their own. This role does not call for drinking, though it is allowed at certain specified times. If the wife consumes alcohol other than at these allowed times, she is considered self-indulgent and irresponsible in her performance of her role. If she becomes an alcoholic, people are shocked. She has very definitely overstepped her boundaries. She has obviously been drinking more than she was expected to. She is found socially unacceptable by the very society which is so tolerant of the man who cannot hold or handle his liquor.

The woman alcoholic is a victim of the double standard existing for men and women. There is a greater stigma attached to her disease than to the same disease in her male counterpart. Instead of being considered sick, she is considered wanton and selfish for drinking the way she does, and even more shame is felt in the families of female alcoholics than in those of male alcoholics. There is a greater tendency to blame the female alcoholic than to understand her when she does not adequately perform her role as wife, mother, and housekeeper.

Our society finds many reasons why a man may drink more than he should. There's his high-pressure job, tense working conditions, monotonous routine, combined business-martini lunches, commuting, demanding wife, unpaid bills. What reasons can a woman have? It's difficult to find any. She's not supposed to be drinking in the first place. Usually husbands and children think her drinking is due to some family problem that will be solved in time. Meantime, however, she should cut or stop her drinking, and she is to blame if she doesn't.

Husbands and children overlook alcoholism as the problem. They do not want to believe their wives and mothers are alcoholics. The idea is very difficult for them to acknowledge and accept even if they suspect it, and they will help her hide her drinking to escape discovery and disgrace. They will exert great efforts to keep her and her problem hidden as long as they can.

The alcoholic wife and mother also suffers acute feelings of shame concerning her drinking. She knows well how society views her. Like her family members she will blame herself, until eventually self-blame and self-recrimination cause a deeper surrender to her addiction. She will keep her drinking a secret for as long as she is able. She will drink quietly and alone; and she will hide it until it can no longer be hidden.

Many wives hide their drinking so well in their early years of alcoholism that when it is finally uncovered it is a genuine shock for the husbands and children. Although it seemed to Ken that Barbara became an alcoholic overnight, the nature and progression of the disease are such that considerable drinking before her last few months was indicated. Upon questioning, Ken could remember behavior indicating that Barbara had been sneaking drinks for several years. Many times Ken had noticed that the bar supply was either lower than it should be or different. Bottles were nearly empty that should have been full; others had obviously been replaced, and some bottles were missing altogether. When questioned Barbara blamed it on the maids or the women who had come to lunch. Ken also remembered that Barbara had stopped drinking at parties or when out to dinner, the only times she had used to drink. Yet she would have alcohol on her breath before going out and frequently appeared tipsy soon after returning home. Barbara no doubt knew she might get drunk, so exerted all her energies toward not drinking in public to escape humiliation and disgrace.

Ken, like most husbands, accepted her explanations even though he did not always believe her. He wanted to believe her. It was too difficult for him to do otherwise. Nor could Barbara do otherwise. Her drinking was as unacceptable to her as to those around her. She was powerless to stop herself, and too ashamed to ask for help.

Nor was there anyone else to help her. Like most alcoholic wives, Barbara did not work outside the home. Although industry and labor have initiated programs to detect and treat alcoholism among their employees and executives, few of these programs cover the housewives as well. They remain isolated in their homes desperately and usually successfully hiding their drinking from the outside world. So they go on unrecognized and untreated.

Husbands do not seem to react in the same ways toward their alcoholic wives as the wives of alcoholic husbands do. They not only have a greater reluctance to accept the idea of alcoholism, but they seem, as well, to have less patience with their alcoholic wives than the wives of alcoholic husbands. This does not mean, unfortunately, they are any more effective in getting their wives to treatment than the wives of alcoholic husbands.

Profiles have been drawn on the responses of wives of alcoholics, and typically most wives respond to alcoholism in their husbands in a way similar to Ellen's. They seem to put up with a lot, at great cost to themselves and to their husbands. Their patience and tolerance, as applied, serve only to prolong the disease and its destruction. Patience and tolerance are certainly laudable virtues to have and are needed in alcoholism, but are of little value unless constructively directed.

Profiles of typical responses of husbands of alcoholics have not yet been clearly established. There is evidence that many husbands act very much like Ellen, putting up with a lot while avoiding treatment for themselves or their mates. Frequently these husbands simply allow their alcoholic wives to live in the house, with little expected of them other than to leave everybody alone. Either the husband assumes the role of mother to his children (along with his role of provider-father) or the role is assumed by an older child. The alcoholic wife and mother is tolerated, but that is all. She is not granted her former roles. Her inability to function has forced others to assume her duties. She is not forced into treatment for her disease, for she is not considered sick or worthy of help, especially if any attempts have been made in the past which proved unsuccessful.

There are indications, however, that most husbands of alcoholic wives do not respond in this manner. More often they abandon their wives. Many will take their children to relatives as Ken did, leaving the wives in the house or in cheaper lodgings. Others will ask the wife to leave and will force her out of the house. And some will desert the entire family, leaving their children to the care of their alcoholic wives and leaving the wives to fend for themselves.

When the husband leaves his family the burden of maintaining the home usually falls upon the older children, who are then deprived of their childhood. Sometimes the husband sends money for their support; frequently he doesn't, or it isn't enough, and the family is forced to appeal for public assistance. The children are usually isolated and ashamed and are fearful of having their peers discover either their mother's drinking or their father's abandonment. They miss school or drop out because they must take care of their mother or because they can't afford the school supplies or because they don't have winter coats. These children may very well carry the impact of the disease of alcoholism on into the next generation, and the next.

Before abandoning their wives, most husbands, like Ken, attempt to control their wives' drinking. They threaten, hide and throw liquor away, withhold money, and a few even resort to abuse. But they have no better luck than the wives who attempt to control their husbands' drinking. Many husbands reduce their wives' work loads and make fewer demands of any kind, in an attempt to eliminate the reasons for drinking. But like their male counterparts, alcoholic wives drink anyway. Many husbands send their wives to psychiatrists, yet the wives continue to drink. Feeling put upon and telling themselves that they've done everything possible—"more than most men would do"—they then feel justified in deserting their wives. On the surface, at least, they seem to feel less responsibility toward their wives and families than do the wives of alcoholic husbands.

When left to their own resources, husbands of alcoholic wives are no more effective in getting them to treatment than are the wives of alcoholic husbands. Society's attitude toward the female alcoholic is a significant factor in preventing her husband from being both more responsible and more effective. Society offers no excuses for her alcoholism. She has not been forced into it by all the extenuating circumstances which society uses as contributing factors for the male alcoholic. If she becomes an alcoholic, it is because she has *chosen* to break a tribal taboo. Therefore she is not considered sick or worthy of help; in fact, she deserves to be punished by abandonment.

This attitude permeates our culture and the husband usually encounters it if he confides in others. Even if he hasn't already crystallized the attitude in his mind, he soon will. He, unlike the wife of an alcoholic husband, encounters very little conflicting advice from families and friends. When the wife of an alcoholic appeals for help, she is given all sorts of opinions and suggestions for dealing with her husband. Some say she should leave him, some encourage her to stay; and all proceed to tell her how to do both differently. Not so with the husband of an alcoholic. He is told, in pretty short order, and almost exclusively (except perhaps by her family) to get out, to get *her* out, to find another wife, to get a mother for his kids who can take care of them properly, she's not worth your worry, and so on. Society, if it doesn't actually support the husband in his desertion of his alcoholic wife, does little in the way of helping him do anything else.

Another factor that contributes to the husband's ineffectiveness in dealing with his alcoholic wife is the fact that most men in our culture place their highest value on their productivity. It is a tragic commentary on our times that most men place more value on their work, their earning capacity and their production, than they do on themselves, their wives, or their children. Most men (and women) do not even question this hierarchy of priorities. Thus, to say the least, husbands do not have as their first priority meeting the needs of their alcoholic wives. The number-one priority lies elsewhere and consumes most of their time and energy. There is very little left at the end of the day to devote to discovering the needs of the drinking wife. Alcoholism is insidious and baffling; it requires considerable time and effort to respond to it effectively. Husbands have more important things to do, or so they think.

Because the husband holds his productivity in such

high esteem, he can tolerate very little interference in this sphere, especially when the interference is coming from the person whose duty it is to assist him in his endeavors. No one has a right to interfere in this area of his life, much less his wife. Many husbands very quickly abandon their alcoholic wives when it looks as if the inappropriate drinking might place their work in jeopardy. Their economic security is, in their minds, enhanced by desertion. The number-one priority rigidly remains number-one; the wife must go.

Husbands are not economically dependent upon their wives. They can afford to leave. They are not locked into their marriages to the same degree that wives of alcoholic husbands are. The wife's need for economic security from her alcoholic husband no doubt makes her appear to be more responsible because she does not desert as readily as she might if she were self-supporting. Either way, economically dependent or independent, husbands and wives are not seeking the help they need and are not responding effectively to the alcoholism of their partners. In that sense, neither group is responsible, and the fact remains: because husbands are financially independent from their alcoholic wives, they are able to effect earlier departures. Abandonment is possible for husbands; it's the easiest out for them and the most expedient. It's also, in human terms, the most costly.

There are many other factors which inhibit the husband's effectiveness in dealing with his alcoholic spouse; mostly they have to do with the nature of the disease itself, and here the husbands are not alone. Alcoholism is difficult for all who are involved with it. When it rains it rains on everyone. But with knowledge and help, it is far from hopeless.

Even though there are many factors working against the husbands (the wife of an alcoholic encounters as many), they are for the most part controllable. The husband can alter the inhibiting factors. It is within his domain to change them if he wishes. By gaining knowledge and assistance he can effectively respond to his wife's disease, just as certainly as if she had TB or diabetes. He can be helped to intervene in her illness, thereby initiating her recovery to the world of health. He can change old approaches and substitute new, constructive ones, thereby avoiding further destruction to himself, his children, and his wife; and he can do it without consuming any more time than he is taking with destructive approaches.

Many husbands have sought knowledge and assistance in approaching the disease of alcoholism, and wives are alive and healthy today because of their efforts. All studies indicate that alcoholic women have as good a chance for recovery as do alcoholic men, once they get to treatment. Female alcoholics get just as well as do their male counterparts, but they have to be reached first.

Husbands! Only you can do it. She has no employer to reach her. She *cannot* reach herself. You are her *only* meaningful contact with the outside world and she desperately needs you to initiate her recovery. *She has a disease—a treatable disease.*

7

THE ALCOHOLIC— HOW THE WORLD VIEWS HIM

When the word alcoholic is mentioned, most people quickly draw an image in their mind of the sort of person they think he is; what he looks like, what he does and where he is. He, first of all, is a he! And quite clearly a shiftless character who cares for neither himself nor the world around him. Every part of him that we can see above, below, and through the tears in his black-brown rags is caked with dirt and old blood; we shudder to think what else might be lurking there unexposed. We find him on doorsteps, blanketed from the winter's cold with newspapers covering his bones, and we think he must not feel in the same way we do. We find him on park benches and in alleyways and skid rows across the country. He shuffles out with an impossibly soiled cloth to wipe our windows for a quarter as we stop for a red light. He seems to have been there always, as if he sprouted forth into this world in exactly that condition.

This is pretty much the preconceived image most of

us have of the alcoholic. It is such a strong image that not only do we believe it to be true, it deludes us into thinking we know something about alcoholism. This image convinces us we know who is an alcoholic and who is not, what alcoholic behavior is like and what it is not like, what an alcoholic's values are and what they are not. We hold to this image with a certainty that makes us blind to who and what an alcoholic actually is.

Only 3 percent of the alcoholics in this country are in the skid rows, and of the people in the skid rows only a small percentage are alcoholics. Our preconceived image of what we are convinced is an alcoholic is perhaps not even based on an alcoholic in the first place. Yet our distorted conception influences our feelings and behavior toward the alcoholics in our midst. It does not allow us to recognize them when we see them or to get them to treatment when we do finally recognize them.

We do not consider the possibility of someone's being an alcoholic if he works, he is young, has never missed a day at work, drinks only beer, makes more money than ever before, does not drink in the morning, drinks only on weekends, goes for weeks and months without drinking at all, or still has his family. If the problem drinker does not fit our preconceived ideas of what an alcoholic is like, then to us he is not an alcoholic.

Unfortunately for the alcoholic and his family, it is not just a small or isolated segment of society that has misconceptions about alcoholism. Almost everyone does, including the doctors, clergy, families, and friends we turn to for help. Even if we expand our own image of alcoholism, we have difficulty finding someone to help us who also has a clear view. Their guidance often reinforces our original misconceived image because others repeat what we already believe. We are not brought any closer to recognizing the problem and finding the solution.

In our minds alcoholism is a moral issue instead of a disease, and as such it carries a stigma which keeps us from recognizing and obtaining help. We are ashamed.

Rather than recognizing the alcoholic's need for treatment, we see his behavior as something he could control if he would. We wonder why he doesn't watch himself more closely. We feel it is a matter of willpower and the inappropriate drinker just isn't applying enough determination. We believe he is weak-willed or lacking in determination. We pass moral judgments and find him wanting. Soon we choose not to be associated with this person or to keep him and his problem hidden.

The alcoholic's behavior helps along the whole process of stigmatizing and moralizing. Alcohol reduces normal inhibitions and allows people to act in ways they otherwise would not—in ways others find acutely embarrassing, disgusting, and even shameful when carried to extremes. And the alcoholic carries to extremes! Under the influence of alcohol he will often do the very things which society deems most improper, thereby seemingly asking for society's value judgments.

He frequently fails to meet either his own expectations or those of others. He makes appointments which he does not keep, he makes promises which he quickly breaks, he starts jobs which he does not finish, his work is excellent one day and shoddy the next, he is tardy and sometimes absent altogether. People regard his behavior as willful irresponsibility instead of seeing it as symptomatic of his disease. They assume he is behaving the way he is because he wants to; they do not see that he has *no other choice*. They believe he should straighten himself up; they do not see him as sick and in need of treatment. The alcoholic cannot be helped when he is approached as a moral issue, yet his very behavior seems to invite that approach. His actions perpetuate the moral stance already in existence.

Although changes are taking place, society has not presented opportunities for families to become aware of the true nature of alcoholism. It is difficult for individuals to move out of their own misconceptions when the society they live in offers them no unbiased information. Families continue to hide their shameful secret, destroying their chances for getting the help they so desperately need, treating the alcoholic with "home remedies" and going it alone.

Society encourages families to act as a unit in managing their own affairs and coping with their own problems. Families are not encouraged to take their problems outside the family unit except as a last resort. Consequently, when the spouses of alcoholics do finally seek help, it is done with reluctance and most likely from other relatives in the larger family unit. They are thus turning to people without the knowledge or skills to help them. Some of the relatives may not want to be involved while others will not hesitate to offer their own "home remedies." As one "home remedy" after another fails, the people who have suggested them very often give up in disgust—often attaching blame to the spouse for not having done "it" right. The spouse then feels guilty, confused, and even more alone.

Frequently the family members to whom the spouse turns feel threatened. They may fear that they will end up with more mouths to feed, going to police stations, or worse, and do not want to be involved any further. After initially trying to help they encourage the spouse to "hang in there and not give up," with assurances that the alcoholic will shape up as soon as the present difficulties are over; or they will advise the spouse to get out altogether. What these friends and relatives are really saying is, "You've made your bed, now sleep in it. It's not my problem, so handle it the best way you can without involving me." Going to friends and family members for help, whether they become threatened or not, serves only to further encase the spouses in the task of dealing with alcoholism all by themselves while adding to their guilt, confusion, and loneliness.

Very few people are knowledgeable about alcoholism. Although the American Medical Association proclaimed it a disease as far back as 1956, many medical schools still do not include it in their curriculum. No schools at all taught alcoholism comprehensively until recently, and many only touch on it today. Some that cover it thoroughly offer the course as an elective only. Yet alcoholism is the third-largest killer in the United States after heart disease and cancer, and there is no doubt that it would be considered the number-one killer if traffic fatalities were taken into consideration or if the correct diagnosis were given on death certificates. The stigma associated with alcoholism is still very powerful indeed.

Although many doctors are knowledgeable about the disease and are very effective in the field of alcoholism, most are still unprepared to deal with it. Many physicians will admit that they are not prepared to treat the alcoholic and will send him to those who are, but unfortunately, there are many who feel prepared even though they have no specialized education in the disease. Alcoholics can drink to their deaths under the care of these doctors because they rarely receive the treatment their disease requires.

With the rapid acceleration in the acquisition of knowledge in almost all the sciences, we have been forced into an era of specialization. There is virtually no profession today which can be mastered in its totality by one individual—each is too vast. The individual must specialize in some very restricted part or area of the larger field—be he a physician, lawyer, or student of literature. As there are specialists for eyes, lungs, nerves, intestines, neuroses, skin rashes, and heart disease, there are specialists for alcoholism. As with any other disease, it is only within the specialization that one can realistically expect to receive the best possible treatment. Putting the treatment of alcoholism under the aegis of one not specialized to treat it will more often than not serve only to prolong the disease and its destruction.

There are many clergymen across the country knowledgeable about alcoholism and involved with its treatment—individually and collectively, from within and from without their discipline. And recently the Catholic

Church stopped granting pledges to people with drinking problems. Since the same people were taking the same pledges over and over, the Church realized that the pledges were abetting alcoholism rather than interrupting it. Today it offers Last Rites, the Sacrament of the Sick, instead of pledges to alcoholics.

The fact remains that organized religion, so frequently turned to by alcoholics and their families, for the most part remains unknowledgeable and unprepared to respond effectively. Most churches have been slow to either initiate alcoholism counseling services of their own or refer their troubled parishioners to alcoholism treatment services in their communities. Organized religion, like the rest of society, has been more apt to offer moral advice, which does nothing to interrupt the progression of the disease.

An alcoholic, being addicted, does not respond to exhortations, nor does he respond favorably to the usual psychiatric approaches, although he is far from sane. If the alcoholic agrees to undergo psychiatric treatment, he is not amenable to it unless he stops drinking, and psychiatrists and other mental health therapists report little success in getting their patients to stop. Therefore, many either do not take them on as patients or refuse to continue treatment if the patient does not stop drinking. Many, however, are truly fooled by the alcoholic who keeps his drinking problem a secret.

Rita's case is not unusual. She started seeing a psychiatrist because she was experiencing an ever increasing state of anxiety. She saw him three times a week for two years before alcohol was even mentioned. "Alcohol was the last thing I wanted to discuss. I didn't know I was an alcoholic, but I was afraid if I told him about my drinking that he would tell me to stop, and I couldn't perceive living without it at that point. So for two years we talked about everything but alcohol; how my cradle was rocked all the way up to my views on Queen Anne chairs." Rita did not really know what she expected from her psychiatrist except that perhaps by some kind of magic the anxiety would disappear with analysis. She also thought he might supply enough pills to reduce the anxiety enough so that she, on her own, could reduce the alcohol which she knew she was abusing. It was not until she finally reached AA that she discovered it was the alcohol which was causing the anxiety in the first place. But until that time she made early morning appointments with her psychiatrist, doused her breath with mouth sprays, and unwittingly demonstrated symptoms of nearly every psychiatric condition ranging from paranoia to phobias, to manic-depressive psychoses, to neurotic character disorders. "As time went by the anxiety increased, the drinking increased, the pills increased, and the symptoms became even more bizarre. Finally, my husband called my psychiatrist to ask what was being done about my alcoholism. My psychiatrist wasted very little time from then on. He told me either to go to AA and stop drinking or to find another psychiatrist. I went to AA, stopped the booze and pills, and all my crazy symptoms and anxieties disappeared. I then started to learn how to live without chemicals."

Like Rita's psychiatrist, many therapists will refuse to treat a person once alcoholism is suspected unless the patient stops drinking, for it is only then that psychiatry can be effective in assisting the patient toward a better understanding of himself and toward a more effective response to living. Many psychiatrists who treat alcoholics recommend that their patients attend AA as well and work in conjunction with that program. Others, unfortunately, do not insist that their patients stop drinking. Although they search energetically for unconscious forces causing their patients to drink inappropriately, in time they are stymied by the drinking itself. As long as they treat alcoholism as a symptom of another disorder, the progression of alcoholism is not interrupted. Little or no help can be offered as long as the patient continues to drink. Analyzing the possible motivating forces underlying the drinking does not seem to help the patient to stop drinking, and the total disease progresses.

Many psychiatrists and other physicians prescribe sedatives and minor tranquilizers in order to reduce a patient's alcohol intake. As a result of the addition of new drugs, the alcoholic has yet another chemical with which to feed his addiction and stands a good chance of becoming addicted to the pills as well. The patient also stands a good chance of inadvertently overdosing either by drinking alcohol on top of the pills or by taking the pills while in an intoxicated state.

Therapists who prescribe minor tranquilizers or sedatives or who allow their patients to drink while undergoing therapy are allowing the disease of alcoholism to progress and are thus performing a disservice to the alcoholic and his family.

A non-mood-altering drug frequently used in the treatment of alcoholics is Antabuse (Disulfiram). Although it is not a treatment in itself, Antabuse definitely has its uses. Normally, when alcohol is consumed it is broken down by the body into acetaldehyde, which in turn is rapidly destroyed before it has a chance to accumulate. When Antabuse is taken, the normal breakdown does not occur and acetaldehyde is allowed to accumulate. Antabuse has no effect upon the body if alcohol is not added, but for three or four days following the ingestion of Antabuse even a minute amount of alcohol will cause an immediate buildup of acetaldehyde—and then the alcoholic is in trouble. He immediately experiences a flushing of the face, neck, and chest, which rapidly turns to a deep red and even purple coloring. With the flushing he experiences a sensation of great heat in the area. This is quickly followed by a pounding headache, which becomes very severe. His blood pressure will rise suddenly, then drop precipitously, producing dizziness, faintness, and acute nausea, sometimes followed by violent vomiting. With all these symptoms the alcoholic will experience a sense of impending death.

Obviously Antabuse is not a drug to be slipped into

the alcoholic's coffee. Before Antabuse is prescribed, the alcoholic must be made very aware of the consequences if he should drink. (In fact, the alcoholic who is taking Antabuse should carry a card with him indicating that fact so that in case of an accident sympathetic bystanders will not give him alcohol.) When the alcoholic is made aware of the effect of Antabuse, it can act as a "chemical fence" between the alcoholic and alcohol. He is deterred from drinking because he knows Antabuse is in his system.

Alcoholics who want to stay sober but do not feel confident about their ability to do so are excellent candidates for Antabuse. Antabuse alone will not bring about the changes a stable sobriety requires, but it can be an important adjunct to the psychotherapy the alcoholic chooses to undertake. Just staying sober—with or without Antabuse—is not enough. If the alcoholic is not committed to making changes in himself, which he cannot do alone, he will sooner or later lose his sobriety, which is dependent ultimately on change.

At the same time, Antabuse is not an effective deterrent unless the alcoholic is himself motivated to stay sober. Spouses usually cannot bring about that motivation by dispensing Antabuse to the alcoholic every morning or by reminding him daily to take it. If the alcoholic wants to stay sober, has hope that he can, yet feels a need for added protection, he will take it. If he wants to drink, he will not take it, will "palm" it if it is dispensed to him, or will drink on top of it.

For those alcoholics motivated to stay sober, but unsure of themselves in the face of crises, Antabuse can bring a freedom from anxieties about drinking. Their decision not to drink is made when they take their morning dose; they can then use their energies constructively rather than wasting them on whether they will or will not drink. On the other hand, many alcoholics are so desirous of staying sober "no matter what" that they feel no need for Antabuse. In the final analysis, motivation is at the heart of the matter.

Very often the need family members have for treatment is overlooked by both the family members themselves and the healing professions to whom they turn for help for the alcoholic. Their problems are overlooked in favor of what appears to be the more serious problem, the alcoholic. A general feeling exists that if the alcoholic gets well, then everyone will be well, but such is not the case. Spouses and children have a desperate need for help, not because they are causing the alcoholism, but because they are in some measure destroyed by it. They need help to regain and maintain their own emotional health, whether the alcoholic is helped or not. By helping themselves they often are directly or indirectly responsible for getting their alcoholic mates to the treatment they need. Yet the tendency exists to overlook the spouses's need for treatment and to concentrate on the alcoholic's need instead; meanwhile everyone becomes increasingly distraught and traumatized.

The stigma and misconceptions associated with alcoholism which so adversely affect our attitudes and approaches to it can be eliminated in time with acquisition of knowledge of the disease based on facts. But that will not be enough. Before society can effectively respond to the alcoholics in its midst, it will have to define more clearly its stance vis-à-vis alcohol usage. Society now responds to alcoholism from within a schism of unreality, viewing alcohol as a social substance but using it as a drug.

Alcohol is an extremely potent drug, affecting the way we think, feel, and act, and that is why it is used. The effect of the drug helps us to relax after a hard day at the office, allows us to be more at ease at a party or intimate dinner or during a sales pitch. Alcohol is consumed to enhance appetites, to reduce appetites, to give us energy, to help us sleep and to perk us up. One glance at a few advertisements in virtually any magazine we pick up shows clearly what effect can be derived from this drug. Virtually any mood is sufficient cause for using alcohol, and that is why we use it—to alter our mood.

Society thinks of alcohol as a harmless social substance, yet uses it and "pushes" it as the potent mood-altering drug it really is. As long as such a schism between ideas and actions exists, there can be no guides or standards for its safe usage. Confusion about what is appropriate and what is inappropriate usage exists, thus confusion about what constitutes an alcoholic and how he should be approached also exists. *Alcoholism is nothing more and nothing less than a drug addiction.* When society does not acknowledge consumption of alcohol as drug usage, the drug dependent person and his family are confronted by naïve thinking and moral judgments. "Why doesn't he drink like other people?" or "Why don't you cut down?" or "I don't get drunk, why do you?" When people deny that alcohol is a drug, they are blind both to its potentially addictive nature and to the actual addiction of the alcoholic. They respond to the alcoholic as if he had control, when in fact he has lost it.

Everyone drinks in our society, or so it seems, and this has an enormous effect upon our attitudes toward the alcoholic. Most adults in the United States drink. Most adults drink safely. The immediate attitude stemming from these facts is that if most people can drink safely, then the alcoholic is going about his drinking wrong. This attitude once again misses the point of the addiction. Once a person has become dependent, and *one out of ten drinkers will,* he can no longer effectively modify his drinking. Once addicted, he no longer has the necessary control to drink safely and must, to save his life, give up drinking alcohol altogether.

The only treatment for alcoholism is abstinence, and people within our drinking society do not look lightly upon abstaining from alcohol. Most drinkers would not want abstinence for themselves and many would even be repelled by the idea. How then can they feel free to advise it for another or to even accept that abstinence is what is needed? Alcohol is readily accessible, it's usage is commonplace and causes pleasurable feelings; it is deemed desirable. To recommend its total abstinence one must assume the role of being a depriving person, while not depriving oneself, which is an unpalatable task for most people. It is far easier to shy away from either the need for abstinence or confronting the alcoholic with that need. Thus people tend to adhere to the moral stance and pass out advice for controlled drinking. While overlooking abstinence, the only effective treatment for his disease, the alcoholic will be exhorted on to bigger and better exertions of the will simply because people in our drinking society are uncomfortable with the idea of total abstinence from alcohol.

The spouses are left alone—ashamed and embarrassed to ask for help; rejected, overlooked, further confused, or not helped when they do seek it. They are forced to cope alone and without established guidelines to follow. If it were a crisis such as a divorce to be coped with, or a death, or a heart attack or a multiple birth or a house to be built, one could go running right out to the local bookstore to buy anywhere from five to ten "how to do it" books. One also could turn freely and without shame to others for guidance and inspiration. Alcoholism, however, is a crisis which neither receives the same attention in the media nor invites open discussion on a personal level. Even if we know someone who has had an alcoholic wife or husband, the chances are that their way of coping involved such destruction that we cannot find anything we wish to follow. Instead of being inspired by those who have gone before us, we perceive futility. Spouses are left to work it out alone without precedents of a constructive nature, without guidelines, and without readily available inspiration and expertise from others.

Alcoholism is an unending series of crises. Divorces end, deaths end, heart attacks end one way or another, houses get built, twins get easier, but the crises of alcoholism go on for years. The never ending crises sap our energies and spirits. We respond to them in ways that erode our self-esteem. The very people who need to be healthy to cope effectively with the crises become sick themselves. Moreover, the sickness that invades the people around the alcoholic is so insidious that the people involved do not even know they're becoming sick. Not only is their own emotional health being undermined, they must respond to a sick person who denies that he is sick and who resists the help being offered. They must somehow, if the alcoholic is to get well, permit him to see and feel his sickness, a task that takes a great deal of emotional strength which the spouse is losing with each passing day. It becomes a case of the blind leading the blind, except that in this case neither party recognizes his own blindness or even that of his partner.

Finally, the alcoholic does not respond to reason. He cannot be reached by appeals to his rational nature, whether one is in evidence or not. People surrounding the alcoholic are robbed of one of man's most effective tools, the ability to apply reason. The alcoholic has one all-compelling need, the urge to repeat the experience of "getting high," which does not respond to reason.

Alcoholics suffer unbelievable tortures—hallucinations, shakes, depression, anxiety, public humiliation, convulsions, and racking dry heaves, to mention but a few —yet they continue to drink undaunted by the very pain their drinking brings about. If the alcoholic had the ability to apply reason, he would certainly profit from his past experiences. If he had the ability to apply reason, he would certainly heed the advice of others who forewarn him of future predictable results of continued drinking. But he is both deaf and blind. The urge to "get high" does not allow him to see the past or listen to the future. The urge to "get high" is stronger than *any* of his senses. Such being the case, he is totally irrational.

In every way alcoholism baffles the imagination and confuses the mind. It breaks hearts and buries spirits. Yet the results of treatment are remarkably good when the alcoholic is treated by knowledgeable and skilled people who are prepared to deal with someone who is sick but thinks he is well; with someone who neither feels a need for treatment nor voluntarily seeks it.

8

THE ALCOHOLIC— HOW HE VIEWS THE WORLD

"That's sick! Just look at him!" Peggy remarked as she and her husband lay in bed watching Jack Lemmon dig up his bottle on the grounds of the greenhouse in the movie, *Days of Wine and Roses,* being replayed on TV. She then went to check on the baby, but detoured into the kitchen where she reached for her giant box of laundry suds on the cupboard shelf. Digging into it she got out a quart of vodka, gulped down a few slugs, recapped the bottle, replaced it in the suds, put the suds back in the cupboard, and returned to her husband with more murmurs of disgust for the TV alcoholic's behavior. It never occurred to her that she was doing exactly the same thing.

John began each day by framing his head with the toilet bowl. Before he could get a drink to stay down he was forced to vomit the two or three he had just gulped. The various physicians he consulted could not find evidence of the "postnasal drip" that John was convinced was the source of his problems. Therefore, while complaining about the incompetency of the medical profession, he continued gulping and vomiting and remained preoccupied with his nonexistent "postnasal drip." It never occurred to him to consider the inappropriateness of his early morning drinking. To John that was not at all unnatural.

Alcoholics do not see things the same way nonalcoholics do. All sorts of different kinds of people become addicted to alcohol, but once the addiction sets in, it is as if these very different people all put on glasses of the same tint and prescription. They all start seeing in a like manner, but in a manner very different from the way the rest of the world sees; and they are all convinced that it is their vision which is true.

The hallmark of alcoholism is loss of control: the alcohol-dependent person's drinking and behavior is frequently different from the way he or she intends it to be. He either drinks more than he intends to, drinks when he intends not to, or behaves while drinking in a manner which he does not intend. He does not have the ability to put his intentions about drinking or behaving into action on a consistent basis. *The chief symptom of alcoholism is denial of the condition.* The alcoholic either accepts as real that which is unreal or rejects as unreal that which is real. Denial in alcoholism is an almost incredible phenomenon. It transforms the alcoholic into a Mad Hatter. He's O.K., everything is under control; it's Alice who's acting a bit strangely.

It all begins at that point when an individual has a drink of alcohol which has a *profound* effect upon him—so profound that he feels a vastly exaggerated sense of gratification. That drink of alcohol becomes a memorable experience of the highest magnitude. The drinker is not an alcoholic yet, but he is a setup for it if he continues to drink. How profound an effect alcohol has upon a person appears to be a strong factor, if not the strongest, in determining whether one becomes addicted or not.

When the individual returns to alcohol he finds his next drink to be as immensely gratifying as the first. He is just as profoundly affected this time and will be as greatly rewarded the next time and the time following that. It is not long before our drinker learns that he will *always,* each time, feel an enormous gratification from drinking alcohol. He begins to feel a pull toward it and returns to it increasingly. Soon our drinker develops a very unique relationship with alcohol, a relationship of implicit trust. He comes to believe in it completely. It always works! *Each* time it has a greatly exaggerated but welcome effect upon him.

Not only does he find that alcohol always works, he also discovers it works the way he wants it to. While he is becoming a slave to alcohol he feels very much its master. He can direct it to do as he wishes. What he can get from one drink he can get more of from two, and more from three. He learns that alcohol can always be relied upon to alter his mood, no matter what it is, to one of being "high" or exceptionally gratified. Our drinker learns well that he can depend upon alcohol; and he soon does.

Each experience of being immensely gratified or of "getting high" solidifies the experiences before it and establishes the groundwork for the ones to follow. As the repeated experiences are reinforced, they are incorporated as a permanent engraving in the drinker's mind. For the rest of his life he will have as part of him a craving to repeat the experience of "getting high." Whenever this craving manifests itself, the drinker will respond to it over food, sex, or even survival.

The alcoholic first receives an immense gratification from alcohol. Why the effect of alcohol is so profound for some drinkers and not others is as yet unknown. The alcoholic, for any number of reasons—not the least of which is the profound effect itself—next seeks that effect. With continued seeking and finding, the alcoholic comes to need the effect. He learns to live with it and in so doing becomes unable to live without it. He will need ever increasing amounts of the drug in order to continue coping, and will ultimately be destroyed by its continued usage. He develops a psychic dependence upon alcohol and a resulting maladaptive response to living. From this point on the course of his life is clearly predictable. If he continues to use alcohol, he will need to keep increasing its usage. It may take many years, but he will ultimately suffer social, marital, emotional, physical, economic, and vocational complications before meeting an untimely death. Once the drinker has developed a psychic dependence, he cannot alter the progression of his disease because he cannot consistently modify his drinking no matter how or what he tries. Total abstinence is his only recourse.

But the early alcoholic or physically dependent person looks O.K. in the beginning years. He remains an accepted member of our drinking culture and drinks within the bounds of what is considered acceptable by his peers. Like them, he seeks his mood swings in more or less appropriate ways, and hides from them any drinking he fears they might consider inappropriate. He is not easily detected at this point, but changes in his drinking are occurring and can be discerned upon scrutiny.

Every drinker, perhaps without even being aware of it, has his own set of rules for drinking which he accepts as being appropriate. When a psychic dependence sets in, the original rules must be changed to accommodate larger amounts and more frequent ingestions of alcohol. Where once our drinker just anticipated times for drinking, now there is an actual preoccupation or urgency to the anticipation, and the alcoholic becomes quite adept at accommodating this urgency. He will break his original ground rules and will do so without a second thought; there is always good reason for it.

"Never in the morning" is a common rule among drinkers. Our drinker has this rule as one of his own and follows it for a time, but then comes the morning his boss suggests slipping out for a "quickie" before the sales conference begins. Our drinker doesn't blink an eye. Without a second thought he follows in the wake of his boss. He does not hesitate at all before breaking his own rule. Following that experience some interesting churning takes place in our drinker's mind: "He drinks in the morning! Where have I been? If he can do it, so can I." Very soon he is faced with another uptight morning situation and recalls his other morning drink. "That drink really helped me out then, I think I'll slip out for one right now." It is not long before he is slipping out for a "quickie" every morning, telling himself, "Everybody does it! One drink certainly isn't going to hurt anybody." He easily breaks his original rule, is not concerned that it has been broken, and perhaps will establish a new rule in its place; "never before ten," for instance.

"Never alone," "never before five," "never on weekends," "never during the week," "only after eating," "never after eating," "never straight," "never mixed" are some other often used rules which drinkers deem acceptable and impose upon themselves. The alcoholic will break such self-imposed restrictions with relative ease and will not bother to re-establish them once he does break them. The new drinking rules that he substitutes are just as acceptable to him as his first set of rules. Nevertheless, they are different from the rules he established originally and are just as easily broken; and in time they will be broken until few rules exist at all.

As his need for alcohol increases there is greater urgency to his anticipation of a drink; he becomes preoccupied with alcohol and develops a rigidity about his usage of it. He becomes progressively less casual about his drinking. Oh, he may act nonchalant enough, but watch his resistance to having a regular drinking time interfered with. Someone who is urgently anticipating a drink does not take lightly any interference with his obtaining that drink. In his early years our drinker could have made the adjustment from planning to have a drink to not being able to have it without distress.

Maybe some displeasure would have resulted but not the acute agitation which he feels today when such situations occur. Now the distress is so great our drinker will go to any lengths to avoid it. As it becomes increasingly difficult for him to tolerate any interference with his drinking, he becomes exceedingly cunning in manipulating or controlling his environment to accommodate his growing needs. He becomes as ingenious at manipulating his environment as he is with breaking his own rules so that he may satisfy his growing need for alcohol. For example, he may now refuse any event or activity that does not include drinking. Since he cannot give that as his excuse, however, he will come up with a whole assortment of explanations: he now finds he's too emotional at weddings (those without alcohol), or "the Joneses never have anything to say"; he "can't stand crowds," or "her cooking is too much to ask of anybody."

When he is unable to dodge a nondrinking or light-drinking situation, the alcoholic loads up with a "few under his belt" before leaving home and, if worse comes to worst, will find a reason for an early departure. Usually, however, he maneuvers extra drinks for himself without detection. A favorite peregrination is to fix drinks for others, thereby gaining a chance for nips or loaded drinks for himself while acting the helpful, friendly guest. Another common maneuver in public places is to feign an "inflamed bladder" or some such condition, thereby getting a stab at the bar for a fast one while supposedly going to the rest room.

The alcoholic sneaks drinks, gulps them down quickly, drinks alone and before or after social engagements, and stops attending functions or gatherings where he knows it will be impossible for him to drink the way he wishes. Before making virtually any decision—be it a new wife, divorcing of an old wife, new client, new town, new job, another baby, new friend, dinner invitation, luncheon meeting, or which flight to catch—he will first ask himself, "What will the drinking be like?" and will then make his decision accordingly.

As his behavior begins to deteriorate with his increased consumption of alcohol, he will be subjected to criticism and attempts at control from others. Instead of reducing his intake of alcohol, he responds by going underground to secrete his supply. Because he feels that his life depends upon getting that drink, he is exceedingly devious and cunning about making sure it will be there. He is able to outmaneuver the most compulsive and thorough of searchers. He hides his supply in every imaginable nook, cranny, and container in all the places where he does his drinking—home, office, or car. The idea of not having alcohol available for any given period of time becomes increasingly alarming to him.

The social drinker crosses the line from social drinking to addicted drinking without being aware of it. He does not perceive the line. The undertow is very gentle in the beginning and our drinker, thinking of himself as a strong swimmer, is not concerned with changes in the current when he does detect them. He has gone from wanting the mood change which alcohol brings about to needing that mood change. He now *must* have the drink at any cost, but he will think of this urge or compulsion for the drink as being the same as in the old days when he only wanted it. He will not recognize the shift from wanting to needing.

Now alcohol has him. He has used it to alter his moods. He has returned to it ever increasingly for the mood alterations and in time his ability to cope has become dependent upon having the mood alterations which only alcohol brings about for him. The more he sought the mood alterations, the more he wanted them; the more he experienced them, the less capable he was of functioning without them. The less capable he was of functioning, the more he came to depend upon alcohol and the resulting mood swing. (At first glance it seems as if a vicious circle has been established, but that is not the case, for it is actually a more ominous downward spiral leading ultimately to the alcoholic's untimely death.)

With increased usage of alcohol there is a price the alcoholic must pay and he will do so willingly, for he cannot perceive living without the effects he gets from alcohol. For example, the alcoholic now sometimes loses control of some of his behavior. He becomes intoxicated or behaves in ways he knows are inappropriate. He feels humiliation, shame, embarrassment— all powerful feelings, indeed, and very uncomfortable for him to tolerate. He can look at these feelings and the behavior that caused them and if he were not addicted he could say, "Hey, I really blew it last night," make a few phone calls to apologize, and make and follow resolutions for acceptable behavior in the future. He could look at the facts, accept his own blame, and take steps to improve. He would remain in touch with reality while dealing with his painful feelings. Such a method doesn't work very well for the alcoholic for long. He is forever "blowing it" and must find different ways of coping with his pain.

Essentially he has two defenses. Both take him out of touch with reality. First, he can repress the whole business. Since recalling it is painful, he doesn't recall it. He tunes it out and thinks of something more pleasant instead. Soon he forgets it entirely and acts as if nothing had happened. People around him can't believe their senses and begin to wonder if maybe they are crazy. Because the alcohol-dependent person represses a great deal, he becomes an expert at just shoving things aside or down. With enough practice he very successfully removes himself in his own mind from those unpleasant experiences his drinking caused. Since he actually *believes* they never happened in the first place, he certainly is not willing to discuss them or to apply anyone else's reason to them. To him they do not exist and he wonders why everyone is making a big fuss over nothing. While people close to him are ready to tear out their hair, our dependent drinker goes merrily on his way.

The second defense the alcoholic has at his disposal and which he *routinely* uses is to rationalize his behavior. If he can say the painful results of his drinking are caused by events or other people's actions, then he can feel better. He does not have to look at his own behavior. His need for alcohol and the effect derived from it do not now permit him to examine his own behavior. To do so might mean giving up drinking and his need to drink is too strong for that. Therefore he applies his intellect, against all reason, to put the blame elsewhere but on his own drinking. The more he applies his intellect to accommodate ever increasing suffering, the more out of touch with reality he becomes. His rationalizations bury his own feelings and he will come to be entirely alienated from them. His rationalizations distort reality and carry him further into an area of misperception. By being out of touch with his own feelings and by misperceiving his world he develops a deluded or impaired judgment, which he naturally does not recognize.

Healthy people also rationalize on occasions, but unless they are overdefended, they have the ability to retrace their own actions back to the original point and assume their own blame. Even little children have this ability. One of my eight-year-old daughters recently messed up on a section of a rug she was laboriously hooking. "You made me do that, Mommy!" was her immediate reaction. When I asked in what way I, sitting across the room, had that kind of power over her, she was able to slowly but surely take her "boo-boos" back to the fact that perhaps she was concentrating on talking rather than hooking. She concluded, "I like to do both. Maybe when I get better at this rug, I'll be able to talk at the same time." Healthy people, big and small, can examine reality and accept it. They are able to profit from their own mistakes.

Alcoholics can neither examine nor accept reality; it is too threatening to them. If they took a look at reality it would mean only one thing: no alcohol. A greater threat does not exist for alcoholics. Their addiction forces them to make and believe their own rationalizations for what is happening to them. The more they rationalize, the more defended they become from the onslaughts of reality, and the more out of touch they are with the world as it exists.

Another price the alcoholic must pay as he progresses in his addiction is a waning of ego strength, or sense of self-worth. This is more ominous than the pain immediately following drinking episodes because it is a pain that never leaves the alcoholic unless he is "high" from alcohol. As his increased consumption of alcohol causes him to be less effective in the various spheres of his life, he develops a nagging but deep sense of inadequacy. With repeated drinking experiences and the resulting inadequate functioning or inappropriate behavior, the feelings of inadequacy mount until they become a chronic self-loathing.

When the alcoholic begins to hate himself, to feel a self-loathing and to sense his own inadequacy, he puts these painful feelings onto others. What he really feels about himself, he will now project onto others. He does this unconsciously, but does it to relieve himself. Now others are "hateful," "mean," "destestable," "slobs," "garbage dumps," "mediocrity," "against me," "spitefull," "disgusting," to list but a few attributes the alcoholic now sees in others as his own ego strength fades. His attitude often becomes one of being superior to all he encounters. He will act as if the world is responsible for behaving toward him in the ways he considers desirable. As his sense of self-worth is sapped, the alcoholic develops a hostile aura and will frequently show his anger toward the people closest to him: the people he is most dependent upon and consequently the ones toward whom he feels the most anger. Because his hostility is often frightening, the people around the alcoholic will frequently assume the burden of guilt dumped on them by the alcoholic.

Barbara was clearly projecting her own feelings onto Ken when she attacked him in her drunken rages. By blaming him, cutting him apart, and accusing him (and everyone else) of being against her she was actually giving vent to her own feelings of self-loathing. She masked her self-hatred by grandiose and defiant attacks on her family. Feeling hate for herself, she felt hate in others. She could not tolerate, even for a moment, Ken's indecisiveness about returning to her. Feeling worthless, she sensed rejection before it was there. Her immediate defense was to project her own hateful feelings about herself onto Ken, as if they were his.

Such feelings of self-loathing are too much for the alcoholic to live with. He gets rid of as many of them as he can by dumping them on others. He gets rid of more of them by creating and believing in an image of himself that is not based on reality. He actually comes to believe he is the person he dreams he is. He does not base his opinion of himself on his actions, but on his thoughts of himself.

Perceiving the self-image of an alcoholic can be an astounding experience when the alcoholic's view of himself is compared to the reality of his present condition. When a patient recently complained about President Ford's pardoning of Nixon, I suggested that it sounded as if the patient would like to to be President. Without a pause he then described what aspects of the presidency would have to be changed before he would consider it. In fact, the patient had not worked in three years and had worked only intermittently the two years prior to that, because he was forever being fired for being drunk on the job. His addiction had rendered him unemployable; it had also forced him to think in a delusional manner. Rather than being able to perceive the facts of his existence, he believed himself to be excellent presidential material. Images based on ideas about himself rather than on the reality of his behavior are more tolerable for the alcoholic; so he builds his sand castles and lives in them without being aware that anything is amiss.

Still, the alcoholic cannot get rid of all his pain. Self-loathing still persists within him, causing great discomfort and even stronger urges to drink. Where at one time he used to drink to feel better than good, he now has to drink to feel just good. Without alcohol he never feels good any more. His massive negative feelings about himself are too great. They cause a constant pain which he can relieve only by drinking.

The alcoholic never feels good for another reason as well, and this one is physiological rather than psychological, but the end results are the same. There is a rebound effect caused by consuming alcohol. The drinker drinks to go up in his mood and goes up because the alcohol he is drinking depresses or puts down certain activities within his brain. After repeated usage over a period of time there exists a heightened agitation level following the depression. What was put down bounces back higher than the original starting point. The alcoholic does not return to a normal physiological agitation level after repeated depressions ("highs" to him) of his brain. He instead bounces back beyond the normal to a level of increased agitation or anxiety; and he *stays* there. When other depressants, sedatives or minor tranquilizers, are used by the alcoholic, they also act to increase the agitation level following the initial depressant action. The very substances the alcoholic uses to reduce his anxious or agitated state serve only to increase it, thereby putting increased demands on him to use them in greater quantities, and as he does so he is forced to employ even more arduously the pain-reducing defenses which take him ever further from reality.

Alcohol also causes brain functioning impairment with resulting physiological memory losses and distortions, which also serve to remove the alcoholic from reality. Periods of temporary amnesia, blackouts, are common to alcoholics. Peggy, the woman with her vodka tucked away in the laundry suds, recalls her first

blackout and her reaction. Both are typical. She remembers having a drink while sitting at her desk making out
a grocery list for a dinner party she was giving the following evening. She next remembers opening the door
to the boy from the store delivering her groceries.
Among the bundles was her shopping list with each
item crossed off in her green ink as it had been selected.
Peggy says "Nothing was missing! I had bought everything on my list, paid for it, wrote out my address for
the delivery, and came home to await its arrival. Little
more than an hour had passed, but it had been a busy
hour and I couldn't remember any part of it. I was mo-
mentarily shocked, but I didn't want to think about it,
so I didn't. I thought instead that it was a neat way to
accomplish an unpleasant task."

Blackouts can range anywhere from a few minutes to
hours and even days. Anything can happen during a
blackout. Our jails are full of prisoners serving time for
crimes of which they have no memory. Blackouts are
frightening to alcoholics and the first thing many of
them do is to check for evidence from the night before.
When they finally find their cars they examine the fend-
ers to see if they've been in an accident, they check
whose bed they are in, they make frantic phone calls to
room clerks for delivery of local papers to discover the
dates and cities they are in, they search thoroughly for
notes they may have written about phone conversations
they may have had. Still, they somehow do not perceive
anything unusual about their behavior. Because they
have blackouts, they assume anyone who drinks beyond
an aperitif has them as well. Some alcoholics do not
even let themselves become aware of their blackouts.
Although they may not always remember getting to bed
the night before, where they have put things, or what
they have said specifically in conversations, they simply
consider these memory lapses normal and will vehe-
mently deny ever having experienced a blackout.

If someone does not remember segments of his life,
he does not have to deal with them, unless of course he

is involved in an accident or some other crisis. Blackouts serve as an additional buffer between the alcoholic and reality.

Alcohol also causes perception distortions which further impair the alcoholic's ability to see reality. The alcoholic can go to a party, slur his words, stumble about, burn cigarette holes in carpets, spill drinks, repeat stories, pass out, and wake up the next morning thinking of himself as the life of the party. What to others is embarrassing, boring, and dangerous is seen as hilarious, scintillating, and daring to the alcoholic. His perception and recall of the drinking episode is impaired by the effect alcohol has upon his brain. When it is suggested that he not drive home, he feels perfectly capable of driving even though he is unable to walk without staggering. What he remembers the next day is what he felt the evening before, that he was perfectly capable of driving and that everyone had made a big to-do over nothing. The effect alcohol has on his brain impairs how he perceives himself while under its influence and how he recalls the experience when sober. Such impaired brain functioning is yet another factor that takes the alcoholic away from reality and into a world of his own.

The end result of all the defenses, distortions, and memory impairments is a massive denial by the alcoholic of his condition. He is rendered incapable of evaluating himself with any degree of accuracy. No wonder it is so difficult to talk about drinking problems to the problem drinker. He can't even relate to the simplest questions about how much or when he drinks. He can only reply by wondering why the question is asked. He feels that surely there is something more important to talk about. Even though the alcoholic's denial is understandable and even expected, I still find myself amazed at its openness. One simple question asked of new patients is, "How old were you when you were drunk for the first time?" and a typical reply is, "I have *never* been drunk!" Quite an incredible response when we consider that the patient is where he is because of excessive drinking and inappropriate behavior.

The alcoholic is drowning, but does not even know he is in the water. He is very sick, but thinks there is something very wrong with the world. He is very scared, but believes he has everything under control, or soon will have. He is in a state of chemical insanity, but because he does not fit the mold of what is generally considered "insane," he is not thought of as such by others.

He is totally irrational and will not get well by any magnificent spontaneous insight of his own. His wall of denial keeps him from that. He will have to be made ready for that insight, and he often can be by skillful handling of the crises his drinking creates.

9

INTERVENTION

Without a message from reality the alcoholic has *no other choice* but to continue drinking. As long as he believes he *can* drink, he *cannot stop drinking*. He cannot stop drinking until he perceives that he has *no other choice* but to stop. For that perception he will have to be confronted with the reality of his condition; otherwise he will not be able to see it. His defenses are too massive and his denial too great for his disease to be interrupted by any spontaneous insight of his own.

As deluded as the alcoholic is, it is possible for him to receive a message from reality telling him that his present line of action cannot continue, that his world is not exactly as he has been seeing it. The message, specially worded and specially delivered by people meaningful to the alcoholic, intervenes in the progression of his disease. The message enables the alcoholic to perceive his sickness; only then is he willing to pursue and accept treatment.

Actually the alcoholic is presented with a message

from reality every time his drinking is inappropriate and causing trouble for himself or others in any way. Each crisis, brought about by his drinking and inappropriate behavior, is a message from reality saying "This is what your drinking is causing." Unfortunately, the nature of the disease is such that the alcoholic does not experience the full impact of his own crises, and it is therefore difficult for him to receive the message from reality contained within them. The defenses of the alcoholic create a wall between him and the world that makes penetration by reality practically impossible. Unfortunately too, the nature of the disease is such that people around the alcoholic keep him from experiencing his own crises fully. They do not allow the alcoholic to participate fully in the very crises he creates; instead, they rescue him. Family members feel compelled to intercede by assuming responsibility for accepting the consequences of the crises. And so usually do employers, colleagues, and even the law enforcement officers who let the intoxicated driver "get away with it."

Sally did not. She allowed Tom to experience his crises. By forcing him to move his own car, pick himself up, cover his own tracks, face being jailed, make his own excuses, she was refusing to rescue him. Since Tom was unable to escape the consequences of his own drinking, he was forced to experience his crises and he was, therefore, in a better position to receive the message of reality which each crisis contained.

The message is there. But every time the alcoholic is rescued from a crisis of his own making, the delivery of the message is intercepted. *Before the alcoholic can receive the message, the message must be delivered.* Family members who seek knowledge and counseling for themselves, and who achieve a stabilization of their own emotional health, are better able to allow the alcoholic to experience his own crises, and be that much closer to treatment. By helping themselves, they are able to help the alcoholic.

Without outside intervention, most alcoholics die of

their disease. Their shield against reality is so great that they are *unable* to perceive their own sickness. Some alcoholics seek help after many years of destructive drinking and it is often thought that these people have in some way experienced a spontaneous insight into their condition. Such is not the case. Rather, they have experienced years of barrages of reality in the form of the crises resulting from their drinking. Crises make attacks on the alcoholic's defensive wall; they do not support it. It is possible, therefore, that enough years of crises will weaken the armor of the alcoholic; then finally a crisis comes along that breaks through it. Very often it is one of the least significant crises which at last brings home the truth to the alcoholic.

But it is dangerous to leave the alcoholic to his own devices, for he is more apt to die than to crack under the burden of his crises, and if he does finally crack it may be too late for treatment to be effective. If the people surrounding the alcoholic take an active stand and do not leave the alcoholic to his own devices, years of suffering, destruction, and an untimely death can in most cases be avoided.

Spouses and other family members who get help in regaining their own emotional health often precipitate crises for the alcoholic without being aware of it. Besides the fact that they no longer rescue him from his crises, their new attitudes and behavior put additional pressure upon the alcoholic. In effect, *their health makes his drinking too uncomfortable for him.* Alcoholics who have sobered up often report that their families' detachment from their drinking made them seek help. They felt so threatened by the loss of control or possible abandonment the detachment signified, that their very fear allowed them to perceive enough reality to feel their need for treatment. Other alcoholics report feeling threatened because their families were living a full life and they could not stand the feeling of being left out.

When an alcoholic recovers as a result of his family's getting help, it is probably a combination of many behavioral and attitudinal changes on their part which finally allows the alcoholic to receive the message from reality. Whatever the reasons, countless numbers of alcoholics are getting well simply because their family members started getting well themselves.

Besides allowing the alcoholic to experience the crises he creates, another effective course of action is to precipitate new crises for him. A new crisis, not of his own making, but a result of all the ones he has created, can force the alcoholic into a corner which has only one door out, and that door opens into treatment. Some families choose to precipitate a new crisis by confronting the alcoholic directly with the facts of his condition, thus indicating his need for treatment and their desire that he seek it.

A skillful confrontation requires knowledge of the disease and some emotional stability on the part of the confronter. It also requires a presentation of facts about the alcoholic's drinking which are concrete and specific. Generalizations will not do in a confrontation; the alcoholic can worm his way right out of them. Judgments and opinions also will not do; the deluded alcoholic is not concerned with that you think; he has opinions of his own that he believes can match yours any day. And if he feels he is being judged, he will immediately become defensive and even less receptive to what you have to say.

If the alcoholic listens during the confrontation, it will be the presented *facts* which catch his ear. The more facts presented, the broader the view of himself he can see and the better the chance for cracking his armor. If the alcoholic listens to the facts, it will be because he feels that the people who are confronting him also care about him, that even though they are saying things that hurt, they are doing it out of concern and not malice. If he listens to the facts it will also be because he does not feel his dignity of being human is under attack, but the acts which he has performed. When the specific acts are criticized, but not his being, the confronting attitude is, "Even though we feel hurt by or don't like certain actions, we care for you." It is under these conditions that the alcoholic will be the most receptive to the message of the reality of his condition.

However, even with knowledge, health, and an appropriate use of the material, confrontations are likely to be most successful if done by more than one person. The alcoholic's defenses are so massive and his resistance to change so great that he may well be able to outmaneuver one person. He will laugh if one person tells him he has a tail. If three people tell him, he may turn around to look.

Ronnie, an attractive, soft-spoken woman in her mid-forties, had reached the point of feeling she could take no more of her husband's drinking. She had attended Al-Anon regularly for over a year and was being counseled at an alcoholism treatment center. Although she felt she had changed enormously, John, her husband, had made no moves toward sobriety, and Ronnie decided she no longer wished to live in an active drinking situation. Her biggest temptation was to pack her daughter and herself and "just leave." Their son was no longer living at home and Ronnie felt she was capable of such a move. Her counselor, while respecting Ronnie's right to leave and her feelings about wanting to escape a dreadful situation, knew she would suffer a great deal of guilt if she made the move without confronting John directly with his need for treatment. The counselor suggested that Ronnie, her daughter, and her son confront John with the facts of his drinking behavior and their desire that he have treatment. If, after the presentation of the facts, John chose not to get help, they could then tell him of their plans for departure.

Although she was afraid of such a confrontation, Ronnie said she would do it. The counselor met with Ronnie's son and daughter to explain the need and the methods for the confrontation. All three agreed to make a list of things that had happened to each of them as a result of John's drinking. They were cautioned to keep the list specific to John's drinking behavior, his actions while drunk. The counselor further suggested, since they were all fearful of John's wrath, that a different person take over immediately with facts from his list whenever John became angry with any one of them. In that way they could more easily avoid succumbing to his belligerence and letting him off the hook.

Ronnie and her children met with John in just the manner suggested, and he did become angry as they all feared he might. But something else happened as well. Halfway through their lists John stopped them by saying, "Please, I can't listen to any more. I'm just no good! I'll leave. You'll all be better off without me." Ronnie's son, recognizing this as one of John's self-pitying moves which he had used in the past to escape painful situations, said calmly, "Dad, this time we want you to hear us out. Kathy had some more on her list and so do I and so does Mom." Ronnie then finished her list and Kathy began again. She described an incident of a month before when a date brought her home and was insulted and berated by her father. She finished by saying, "Dad, he is the valedictorian of his class and you were so drunk you fell onto the end table and knocked it over. I liked him, Dad, and he never called me after that night." John sank back into his chair and doubled over with deep, racking sobs. After a few moments, tearful himself, the son asked in a quiet but firm voice, "We love you, Dad. Will you go for help?" John continued sobbing but nodded and said softly, "Yes, I'll do anything you wish. I never knew it was so bad." The change was dramatic. Where but a few moments earlier he had been in a rage, albeit a silent rage, he now felt and expressed gratitude for their concern. The various options open to him were discussed and John, preferring not to go to a hospital, elected to attend AA. The family accepted this choice with the understanding that he would go to a hospital for detoxification and rehabilitation if he should start drinking again. As it turned out he received all the help he needed in AA and never required additional treatment.

By being forced into a corner where he had to look at the reality of his drinking behavior, John perceived his need for treatment and became willing to pursue it. A friend of mine went through a similar experience with her husband, but under different circumstances as she had no children to help her. Margaret's husband, Gary, who had tried AA, would stay sober a few weeks and then go off on a bender whenever he was away on business. After a particularly bad binge she received a long-distance call from Gary asking her to call AA in the city he was in to help him get on a plane so he could get home. Margaret did so and then asked a local AA friend of Gary's to help her confront Gary with his need for hospitalization. Upon his arrival, Gary promised he would do it AA's way this time and if that did not work he would go to a hospital. Within weeks, however, the incident was repeated, and this time Margaret reserved beds in both the detoxification and rehabilitation units of an alcoholism treatment center. When she and the same AA friend met Gary at the airport, Gary was again sure he could do it with AA. "I know what I did wrong," he said. "Now I know what to do. The next time I have to travel I'll contact AA out there in advance." Margaret and the AA'er shook their heads and said, "You had your chance to do it your way, Gary. We're now going to let you keep the promise you made to us last month." They then drove an angry and protesting Gary right to the hospital from the airport.

Gary says it took him about two weeks to appreciate their action and to see how much he needed the treatment he was getting. He has been sober for over a year now and has become active in getting other alcoholics to treatment. In his turn he was recently asked to meet a drunk falling off an airplane. "The guy chose AA, but you can be sure if he drinks again we'll be at the airport to meet him and hold him to his promise of going to the hospital. It saved my life, maybe it will save his."

Richard, a dignified banker in his fifties, went to a lawyer to start divorce proceedings after nearly twenty-five years of marriage. The lawyer heard Richard out and then asked permission for an interview with Kay, Richard's wife. After his meeting with Kay he spoke to Richard of her apparent alcoholism and need for treatment. He suggested that Richard set up a meeting for both of them as soon as possible with an alcoholism counselor. The counselor struck at Kay's alcoholism and left it to her to decide what was to be done about her illness. Three choices were presented: treatment at one of several hospitals, joining Alcoholics Anonymous, or denying the problem and having the marriage end in divorce. Kay chose to attend AA with the understanding that if this was not successful she would submit herself for hospitalization. In the meantime it was suggested that Richard attend Al-Anon. They have since begun to re-build a marriage that would have been destroyed had they not encountered a lawyer both knowledgeable about alcoholism and committed to its treatment.

Parents also can be effective in getting help for their children by boxing them in a corner where treatment is offered as the only acceptable way out. Ginny was twenty years old, a former heroin addict and now an alcoholic. Because she was having trouble making a go of it by herself she moved back to her parents' house, causing enormous disruptions and worry for her family. When they sought counseling it was suggested they not condone Ginny's drinking by allowing her to live with them if she continued to drink. Ginny's parents told her they wanted to help her and would pay for her hospital-ization, but if she continued drinking and chose not to go to the hospital she could no longer live at home. Ginny angrily stormed out of the house with a few choice words for how she felt about her parents. Two days later she returned, bruised and sick. She agreed to go to the hospital when it was offered again and was admitted that day. Upon completing treatment at an alcoholic rehabilitation center, she went to a facility for extended care, where she plans to stay for a year or longer. While receiving treatment she is completing her high school education and is making arrangements to enter college in the fall. Her parents' firm stand gave her no real choice but to accept treatment. She now has another chance at life.

Employers can often be even more effective in intervening in the progression of alcoholism than family members can. Quite simply, the alcoholic grants his employer more power than he grants his family. Alcoholics, like so many others in our society, place a higher value on their productivity than they do on themselves or their family. Consequently the alcoholic feels threatened at the thought of losing his job and will muster all his will to control his drinking in that particular sphere of his life. But sooner or later he loses his control and his performance on the job will begin to suffer. He can then be detected and motivated to go for treatment.

Employers are not as reluctant to take constructive action as are family members. Being less involved emotionally, they can respond with more objectivity. And because the alcoholic grants them more power, they have the most leverage over him. Thus, although they are usually the last to know, informed employers are often the first to take constructive steps to intervene in the alcoholic's disease.

The most meaningful people to the alcoholic are his immediate family members and his employer. They are usually the only people who have sufficient concrete, factual, and specific data for effective confrontations. They are also the only people who exert enough leverage over the alcoholic to get him to treatment. The greatest service these meaningful people can do for the alcoholic is to force him to go for treatment. Anything else is cruel and unjust.

Many people will say it isn't fair to force a person to go for treatment, and furthermore "it won't work that way." Yet we do not let these arguments stop us if a relative or employee is hemorrhaging, has TB, or has a ruptured appendix and is reluctant to go to a hospital. We cart him off regardless of what he wants, and he gets treated in spite of himself. The same can hold true for alcoholism. *Alcoholics who are forced into treatment against their will have as good a chance at recovery as those who go more willingly.* Further, the recovery rate for alcoholism is exceedingly high when compared to the rates for other chronic physical or mental conditions.

10

EMPLOYERS

Companies, both large and small, unwittingly have an unwritten policy on alcoholism. It is the result of the effects of the social and moral stigma associated with alcoholism on the attitudes and customs of most company personnel. If written in typical company language, it would read something like this: "This company will award cash and other economic premiums to any employee who can successfully conceal his alcoholism from the attention of management. Such premiums will include sick-leave pay, job security, fringe benefits, and promotional opportunities. When the employee can no longer conceal his alcoholism, his employment will be terminated." This unwritten policy, of course, does not solve the problem. Yet all companies are guided by it and will continue to be until they replace the unwritten policy with a separate written policy statement on alcoholism that does work. Until that time, everyone loses. Business and industry lose an estimated $15 billion annually. Unions lose through disgruntled membership, increased grievance disputes, lengthy arbitrations, and loss of members who become unemployable. Alcoholic employees lose their opportunity for a meaningful existence, and ultimately, they lose their lives.

Beyond that, the unwritten policy is terribly uncomfortable to execute. Under it, supervisors (and managers) are forced to warn and threaten, deny and conceal, plead and cajole, feel embarrassed and ashamed, and endure one broken promise after another. They are thus degraded and quite naturally develop resentments and frustrations that in turn affect their own job performances.

Michael's superiors were at a loss. Nothing they were doing with Michael was working, yet they felt they were doing everything they could. Later, when Michael died during a hemorrhaging episode not long after his forced resignation, the officers of his firm were saddened but at the same time felt, because they had not been successful, that Michael had been a hopeless case. Actually it was the actions dictated by their unwritten policy on alcoholism that were hopeless.

Michael was considered a brilliant lawyer and his firm did not want to lose him. For many years it was fairly easy to ignore Michael's downhill progression. There were several times when his judgment was poor, his behavior inappropriate, and his time unaccounted for, but this seemed insignificant when contrasted to his still brilliant resolution of so many cases. Also, no one knew how else to deal with him. For the most part his colleagues and senior officers were embarrassed, even ashamed, to speak to Michael about his drinking problem, so they overlooked as much as possible. When they could not ignore Michael's inappropriate behavior and were forced to speak to him, Michael either insisted that drinking had nothing to do with what was going on or else pointed to his successes as if they somehow made up for his inadequate performances. He made direct confrontations very difficult and members of his firm would back off for the moment, remembering his assets and forgetting his liabilities.

As time passed and his alcoholism progressed, Michael could no longer insist as adamantly that his drinking had nothing to do with his difficulties, nor did he have as many successes to point to. He would try to put the blame elsewhere, on his family or clients or office staff, but would ultimately promise to "cut down" and to "pull myself together," ending each time with the assurance, "I'll be all right."

Of course he was never able to pull himself together. His senior partners, guided by the unwritten policy and thinking they had done more than their share with all the "chances" they had given Michael, eventually reached their limit and asked him to resign. Although suggestions to seek treatment were made on several occasions, treatment was never offered as a firm alternative to the disciplinary action warranted by his unsatisfactory performance.

Alcoholism is not new; it has been around since the cave man first discovered the fermented apple. Effective approaches to alcoholism, however, are new. Attempts to help alcoholic employees originated in the 1940s, when a few employers started offering treatment to those alcoholics they could easily spot. Right from the beginning, the alcoholics thus referred to treatment responded to the treatment received; 60 to 80 percent achieved long-term, stable recoveries—an incredibly high percentage for a chronic and fatal disease. Treatment was never a problem, nor is it today. Detection and motivation are the problems, and in these two areas the industrial alcoholism programs begun in the forties fell short. They neither discovered nor motivated to treatment the vast majority of their employed alcoholics.

To be detected is the last thing an alcoholic wants; therefore he uses enormous energies to conceal his abnormal drinking. He will go on with his act of "drinking like everyone else" even when he can no longer hide his shakes, sweats, flushed face, bloodshot eyes, and staggering gait. By then he is easily detected by anyone; but then he is in the final phase of his illness. Right through the 1940s, 1950s and into the 1960s, alcoholism was thought of, rather as a self-inflicted condition and a moral problem, and no one in those years was considered an alcoholic unless he came close to the skid-row stereotype. It was therefore these late-stage alcoholics, no longer able to hide their advanced symptoms, who were being reached by the early industrial alcoholism programs. The alcoholics who were not yet in their late stages were remaining successfully hidden in the general employee population.

Awareness of the two problems, identification and motivation, intensified in the mid-1960s, when extensive in-plant industrial studies were undertaken over a five-year period by the National Council on Alcoholism in several large multiplant corporations. Among other things, the thick personnel files were examined, and what a story they told! One such employee's files revealed the following signs of failing job performance over and over for the last fifteen years of his employment: absent, late, warned; sick with "flu," absent, late, warned; vacation days taken individually and without prior notice; sick with "the virus," late, warned. And still it went on—not getting along with fellow workers, spurious and suspicious excuses for poor workmanship, warned; "frozen toes," hospitalization for amputation of toes; alcohol on breath, suspension; transfer to new department; extended lunch hour, asleep on job, terminated; reinstated; late, hospitalization for "high blood pressure," poor workmanship, warned; staggering gait, final termination. File after file, year after year, the same symptoms. This survey led, in the late 1960s, to industrial alcoholism programs that concentrated on the signs of job deterioration rather than those of alcoholism.

Roger was the beneficiary of one of these new and

more effective programs. Being a chemist and loving his chosen work, Roger began his career with high hopes. His achievements were great in his early years; then he changed, slowly but surely. Where at one time he was popular with his colleagues, Roger became argumentative and easily slighted. As the people around him withdrew, he became suspicious, thinking others were talking about him and deliberately making his work more difficult. In time Roger became increasingly irritable during the morning hours, barely speaking to anyone, yet unexpectedly voluble and jolly in the afternoons, ever eager for an ear to bend. This change in sociability did not bring about friendship with his colleagues, however. Although jolly, he was boring, often repeating himself. His co-workers considered this behavior no more desirable than his icy morning withdrawals. Nor did his work improve. In fact, it became hazardous to work in the same laboratory with Roger. Both states, the morning irritability and the afternoon sloppiness, caused Roger to break equipment, spill chemicals, and bump into ongoing experiments.

Previously the supervisor in such a situation was placed in a difficult spot. Not only was he told to diagnose people unwilling to be diagnosed, using a grossly incomplete symptomatology chart as his guide, he was also told to "do something" about the alcoholic—to counsel him—once he made his diagnosis. Alcoholics are difficult to deal with, even by those with special training. They are accomplished manipulators. They are forced to be; their addiction must be fed. The average supervisor, well prepared to be both "firm and frank" and "sympathetic and understanding," was soon outmatched. He found himself accepting the alcoholic's convincing tale of woe. His resulting attitude was often one of sympathy—"My God, I might drink too, under those circumstances"—and the resulting action, granting "one more chance," was far from being firm. The alcoholic won another round, the supervisor suffered nagging feelings of having been used (he had been, of course), the illness progressed, the job problems continued, and the problems of early identification and motivation to treatment were not met.

Today's effective industrial alcoholism programs do not impose the role of diagnostician and counselor upon the supervisor. Today he does what he is trained to do in the first place: monitor the job performance of those under him.

Roger's department head had concrete factual data about Roger's substandard performance. In his meeting with Roger he listed the examples of Roger's poor interpersonal relationships (all very different from the way he once was); the instances of errors, spillage, breakage; and the abrupt personality change that occurred each afternoon. When Roger attempted to rationalize his unsatisfactory job performance, his supervisor kindly but firmly stated that he was only interested in restoring performance to an acceptable level, but that if Roger wished help for whatever it was that was causing him difficulty, he could in complete confidence seek help from the counseling, diagnostic, and treatment services offered by the company. Roger refused to accept this service, saying he could handle it alone. The supervisor said, "Fine, I hope you can, because we are concerned. We expect your performance to return to its former acceptable, in fact excellent, status."

And Roger did bring his performance up to par. He was not exactly the friendliest chemist around, but he worked competently and less garrulously for a while. Then his performance took an abrupt change for the worse and Roger returned to his former state, in which his colleagues again considered it hazardous to work with him. This time Roger's supervisor approached him differently. The examples of his poor workmanship were again described but Roger was told that he must now make a choice between either the professional help offered or the disciplinary action appropriate to his unsatisfactory performance. He was reminded, "You were given the offer of help before, which you refused on the premise that you could do it yourself. That has not worked out. This time we again offer you help and, if you accept, your job will not be in jeopardy. However, if you elect to refuse this offer of help we will then take the appropriate disciplinary action in response to your recent inadequate performance pattern." Roger was furious but he had no real choice. His only viable option was to agree to seek the help offered.

The system is simple. When an employee's performance drops below acceptable standards, and when regular corrective procedures fail to restore acceptable performance, he is referred to professional diagnostic and counseling services for identification of the problem, followed by treatment appropriate to whatever the problem is.

Naturally, not all substandard work performances are due to alcoholism, but usually 60 percent or more of the cases are. Alcoholism alone is accountable for more impaired job performances than all the other medical-behavioral problems combined. Sooner or later the alcoholic's addiction interferes with his ability to produce on the job, thus all alcoholics suffer impaired job performance as their disease progresses. When all employees with deteriorating work records are referred to diagnostic and counseling services, the alcoholics are identified and treated in the early or middle phases of the illness, before it becomes more costly to themselves, their families, and their employers. At the same time, the non-alcohol-related problem cases are served as well. And supervisors no longer have to get involved in the diagnostic and counseling functions. This is left up to those trained to do it, the professionals operating the company's alcoholism program. Members of management have to do only with what is the proper and legitimate concern of management.

Supervisors often wonder what the real difference is, because they realize they still have to confront the alcoholic. The vital difference is that now all the supervisor has to discuss with the employee is the fact that his performance is substandard. Like Roger's supervisor, he simply describes specifically how the performance is substandard and then offers the employee the opportunity to seek confidential help from the company's program director or an out-of-company resource, without jeopardizing his job, in case a problem of any kind is bothering him. The supervisor does not have to talk about causative factors at all. He does not have to discuss alcoholism. He does not even have to know what the problem is. He simply offers help in case it's needed and at the same time asks that the employee bring his job performance back up to standard. It is not his concern whether the employee seeks the assistance offered or not.

At the second or third corrective interview, however, it becomes his concern. Now, like Roger, the employee no longer has a choice. He must accept either the original offer of help or the consequences established by the company for unsatisfactory performance. Usually this means his job is on the line, through either suspension or discharge.

At this point, thinking that this is the kind of interview they could happily do without, supervisors often ask, "What if he refuses? How do I get him to go for help?" The answer is, "You don't! He gets himself to go." The choice is clearly his. It is not in any way up to the supervisor to talk him into going by either salesmanship or pleading. The supervisor simply presents the choice as Roger's supervisor did and then sits quietly back. He lets the employee feel the impact of the "treatment or else" offer. He does not dilute it with words and, above all, he does not enter any discussion with the employee about the causes of the poor job performance. He announces that the employee's job performance is not acceptable and that now he must either get help or accept the consequences of refusing help. (Nonalcoholic troubled employees would long ago have accepted the offer of assistance.) The interview is then quickly and quietly concluded by setting a time for the employee's consultation with the professional diagnostician-counselor. This second or third interview, frequently the one most dreaded in the beginning, is very often the easiest and most satisfying one of all.

But, as with Roger, things are not so quiet within the alcoholic. He is very angry, although afraid to express it, and he begins immediately to plan how to con the professional consultant until the heat is off. Once in consultation, he is out-matched. None of his manipulations will work and he will be directed to the treatment appropriate to his needs, *and all because he wants to keep his job*.

The same desire will motivate him to continue treatment. Once treated and once the recovery process begins, the alcoholic's hostile attitudes are replaced with attitudes more conducive to harmonious relationships. Almost without exception, treated alcoholics return to work with feelings of gratitude toward the very persons they once so deeply resented for forcing them to treatment in the first place. This is truly a rewarding and meaningful experience for both the supervisor and the employee.

Roger effected drastic changes very quickly. Because of his enormous denial and resistance to recognizing his need for help, the program director recommended that Roger be hospitalized. Once again Roger knew he could not refuse because to do so would mean losing his job. Once in treatment he was confronted heavily with the reality factors of his alcoholic existence. The defenses that kept him out of touch with reality were described and new methods of coping were developed. At the same time he was subjected to an intensive didactic education on his disease. Within two weeks, Roger gave up. He recognized the totality of his condition and accepted it. He then could and did begin to assume responsibility for his own recovery. When he was discharged from the hospital, he joined his company's after-care program and became an active member of AA. Once again he was a responsible employee, very grateful for the opportunity given to him by his company.

If the alcoholic chooses to refuse the help offered to him by his employer—only about one out of a hundred will refuse—the interview is still the same. His choice to be fired is quietly accepted without any attempt to make him change his mind, and he is referred either to personnel or whoever handles the next action or it is handled by the person doing the confronting, whichever is standard company practice. Even this choice, and the employer's follow-through on it, may save the alcoholic's life. Now he has no job. He can no longer tell himself, "I'm not an alcoholic! I'm still working." This is frequently the last defense for alcoholics, and its removal allows many to seek help for their disease. Meanwhile the best interests of the company are served as well.

The "treatment or else" choice is extremely effective. It is, in fact, the strongest motivating factor that exists. When confronted with it, alcoholics elect treatment. They elect treatment for all the wrong reasons, but nevertheless they elect treatment. Alcoholics can be helped whether they want help or not, once in treatment. Out of every ten alcoholics referred to treatment with the "treatment or else" choice, six to eight return to their jobs with successful long-term recoveries.

Not all alcoholics make it the first time around, as Roger did, although most do. Some, like Walter, start drinking again. Walter worked as a mechanic in a unionized plant. Like Roger, he accepted (reluctantly) the services offered, which in his case consisted of counseling within his company by the program personnel and AA in his community. It was decided that he did not require hospitalization. Walter responded to treatment for five months, but only five months. After four months he dropped out of his counseling sessions and presumably out of AA, and soon after that his performance on the job fell back below standard.

He was then confronted by both the shop steward

and his supervisor. The examples of his poor job performance were described and Walter was asked to take a one-month leave of absence without pay. The shop steward told him his job could not be protected since he was not cooperating with treatment. (Naturally, it would not have mattered at all whether Walter cooperated with treatment if his job performance had not suffered.) Both interviewers told him that if he got back into treatment his job would be there for him in one month.

Walter returned to treatment and then to his job, and made a stable recovery. The lines were clearly drawn for him. He knew very well that if he drank again and his work suffered (as he knew it would if he drank) he would then get a three-month leave without pay, and after that, if he still did not effect a recovery, he would be out of a job. His one-month leave of absence had already told him his company and his union meant business and could not be manipulated. He too was forced to get well.

This is the way successful industrial alcoholism programs work. Alcoholics are both identified and motivated to treatment earlier in their disease process. But there are not nearly enough such programs. Industries, because they control the two most effective motivating tools available, the paycheck and education, are in a unique position to reach millions of alcoholics. The National Council on Alcoholism reports, however, that of the 1,600,000 American corporations now in existence, only about 600 to 700 have adopted some form of alcoholism program. Of these existing programs, which cover only a small portion of the employed alcoholic population, only a small percentage utilize the modern approach and methods just described, and no more than 25 to 30 of these are achieving anything near their potential in terms of early identification and successful motivation to treatment.

As more is known about how costly alcoholism really is to industry, and how easily, inexpensively, and successfully it can be combated, alcoholism programs should begin to proliferate. For example, a recent study undertaken by the National Council on Alcoholism has found that the job performance of employees who are not themselves alcoholics, but who have an alcoholic in their home, suffers as greatly as if these employees were themselves alcoholics. This study contributes significantly to the realization that alcoholism is costing industry even more than previously estimated. The study also indicates that any successful industrial alcoholism program has to be available to family members as well. Thus, industry's potential impact on alcoholism detection and motivation to treatment, already great, becomes even greater.

The best alcoholism programs are available not only to family members but to any employee who wishes to seek help on a voluntary basis. Family members and employees can refer themselves for any problem, and when they do, it is a purely private matter between them and the program personnel. No one in the company is notified that the employee or family member has sought help. (When the employee is referred by a supervisor, the supervisor is then told whether or not the employee has kept his appointment and whether or not he is cooperating with treatment. Beyond that, the utmost confidentiality is maintained in these cases as well.) Consultations and treatment are confidential, unless, of course, hospitalization is needed which is to be covered by the company's insurance plan. If sick time is required, the immediate supervisor is notified, but is not told of either the diagnosis or the treatment unless the employee chooses to give out that information himself.

A successful alcoholism program establishes itself, in time, not only as an effective source for help but also as a "safe" source. When programs start, most referrals are from supervisors. As time passes the proportion of self-referrals increases, often by more than five percent a year. Employees who have been helped spread the word. Others begin to realize that they too may be able to be helped, and they appeal to the same "safe" source that has helped their co-workers. The supervisor of an assisted employee often joins the employee in becoming one of the program's best salesmen.

Within every company there is always a certain number of employees who are not closely monitored. Often these employees are members of top management, who, though they escape a direct type of supervision, do not escape alcoholism. Frequently too, these people are surrounded by colleagues who, for reasons of their own, "cover" for them. Intervention is not as easily made available to employees who hold positions of power and are not closely monitored. When company alcoholism programs are considered both "safe" and effective, many of these alcoholics will seek help on their own.

Alcoholism programs will not be successful without the active involvement of any existing unions. Some companies wanting an alcoholism program are unable to establish one because of union opposition. On the other hand, some companies have alcoholism programs simply because unions insisted upon them as part of their collective-bargaining package.

In the words of Leo Perlis, AFL-CIO community services director, "Alcoholism programs are neither pro-management nor pro-labor, but pro-people." A sound alcoholism program benefits both labor and management. Unions reduce the number of grievances and arbitration proceedings and management reduces its costs. Unions protect the true job security of their members and management regains effective employees. Both save lives. Wider acceptance of alcoholism programs among unions is expected as they become more aware of the benefits they stand to gain as well as the cruical role they can play in serving their membership.

When a company is establishing an alcoholism program, it is important to remember the need for a separate written policy statement on alcoholism. Although alcoholism is the most serious health problem any company has, it has routinely been left out of company health benefits. The only way to counteract the stigma of alcoholism is to attack head on, to call it what it is, a disease, and treat it with the respect it deserves. A separate, written policy statement is the beginning. The joint Union-Management Committee of the National Council on Alcoholism, co-chaired by James M. Roche, recently retired chairman of General Motors Corporation, and George Meany, president of the AFL-CIO, has established a comprehensive guideline that reflects the broad principles of a successful alcoholism program. Obtainable from the National Council's New York headquarters, this guideline stresses the need to recognize alcoholism as a disease and to have top-level joint union-management involvement, with a joint union-management written policy statement on alcoholism. It discusses, as well, the principles for inclusion in the written policy statement and the principles for implementing the policy.

The basic unit, employer-employee, is the same for any successful alcoholism program, whether the business is very large or very small or in between. A successful program is feasible for any size as long as the basic unit of employer-employee exists.

Having been on the receiving end, so to speak, of many industrial alcoholism programs whose employees I have treated, I take this opportunity to share my experience with all of you, but most especially with those of you who are employers, supervisors, members of top management, shop stewards, and union officials. We in the treatment services take up where you leave off. We get your employee with his enormous resentment for being forced into treatment. But because he is determined to manipulate us as he tried to manipulate you, and to put in his time and then "get the hell out," he either keeps a very low profile or volubly describes how much he wants and needs treatment, which he then proceeds to "prove" by speaking of his "voluntary" admission, as if he had about ten other viable options. What he does not realize is that before he is admitted we establish from the referring person just exactly where this patient stands vis-á-vis his job. When we know his job is unequivocally on the line, we can attack this denial system immediately and he can then begin to engage himself actively in the treatment process. As a result, we can usually send back to you a "grateful to be alive and sober" alcoholic prepared to begin assuming his share of responsibilities. On the other hand, if the patient's job is not on the line, he is more resistant to engaging himself in the treatment process. These patients are usually very cooperative and comply with the program, but they do little else. They often resemble the student observers who pass through as part of their education. They do not feel compelled to be patients. The energies they could be using on self-examination are used instead on maintaining this "passing-through observer" role. Quite simply, they know they can drink again and "get away with it." And when an alcoholic believes that, he feels little need to take his treatment seriously.

I treated eight patients in the past year from one company whose policy seems to be to transfer the alcoholic to another department (sometimes up) when his performance once again deteriorates following treatment, which in treatment language is when he drinks again. Seven out of eight of those ex-patients are still drinking, their disease is progressing, and they are all still employed at the same company, albeit in ever rotating departments. Some of them may die before their job is put on the line.

This kind of paternalism or protectiveness, either inherent in the company or imposed on management by labor, though well meant, definitely falls into the realm of "killing with kindness." A hard-line approach is necessary in alcoholism. The sooner management and labor recognize this need, the sooner lives will be saved, costs reduced, and jobs protected. Alcoholics can be helped, and aside from humanitarian reasons, it is just plain good business to do so.

11

FAMILIES AND
FRIENDS

A natural law exists in all close relationships: *If one partner makes a change, the other partner
must accommodate to that change with changes of his
own to balance the relationship, else it ceases to exist.*

When a change is made by one of the partners in a
relationship, the change is either helpful or not. If it is
helpful it serves the person well, and holds the potential
for serving the partner well, depending on the partner's
reaction to that change. If the change is harmful, it hurts
the person effecting the change and is potentially
damaging to the partner, depending on the partner's
reaction to that change.

In alcoholism the natural law of relationships has a
good and a bad aspect. *Alcoholics make changes that
are destructive. Partners of alcoholics also make
changes that are destructive* in their attempts to restore
the physical, emotional, and spiritual norms of the relationship. In so doing they become as much a part of the
maladjustment of alcoholism as the alcoholic. They of-

ten suffer as acutely as the alcoholic. Partners of alcoholics have a choice, but are rarely aware of it.

Alcoholics change as their disease progresses, slowly,
subtly, inexorably and eventually drastically—and *the
changes are always harmful.* The changes the alcoholic
makes hurt him. The changes hold the potential for
hurting his partner, depending on her reaction. Whether
the partner gets hurt or not will depend upon whether her
reactions are constructive or not; whether they serve
her well or whether they don't.

If the partner's reactions serve her well by meeting
her rational self-interests, they increase her sense of
self-worth and effectively counter the alcoholic's original harmful actions. If the partner's reactions are destructive, they do not meet her own needs, and thus allow the alcoholic's actions to be hurtful.

Contrary to what the spouse thinks, the alcoholic
cannot hurt her unless she allows it. But the spouse
(male or female) would have to be superhuman not to
fall into the trap of responding negatively to destructive
changes in the alcoholic. Without knowledge of the disease it is virtually impossible to do anything else.

Alcoholism is baffling, spouses don't know what
they're dealing with; it's threatening, they never know
what to expect except that it will probably be bad; it's
ugly and shameful, they cannot deal with it openly.
Spouses respond, therefore, the best way they can, in
ways that have worked before and that are natural to
them. But with alcoholism, they find they are all alone
in a strange, inhospitable land where their old ways do
not work. Not having received training in ways that do
work, they continue with the old and succumb to the
disease.

The spouse responds to harmful changes in the alcoholic with harmful changes of her own which hurt her
and which are, in turn, potentially damaging to the alcoholic. Being maladaptive, the alcoholic responds negatively thereby increasing his own destruction and providing more potential for the spouse's destruction.

The responses of Ken and Barbara are an example of destruction feeding upon destruction. As Barbara's drinking increased, she was unable to perform adequately as a wife and mother. The changes she was making were certainly harmful. Ken, being uninformed, felt her changes were deliberate and responded negatively by temporarily abandoning her. His reactions did not make him feel good about himself, nor did they meet his rational self-interests. His negative reactions did not effectively counter hers, and he suffered because of it. Barbara responded to Ken's reactions with increased drinking, which led to increased destruction and severe personality changes resulting in vicious attacks on Ken. Feeling personally attacked—it certainly looked like that on the surface—he reacted destructively by deserting Barbara completely, except for weekly stipends which she used to buy booze, which led to her premature death.

Destruction breeds destruction. It's a whirlpool—a deadly one, wide and relatively gentle at the top and narrow and vicious at the bottom. The harmful changes and negative responses gather momentum, causing both partners to suffer a gradually narrowed range of options until both are acting out of compulsion rather than choice. They come to know and have at hand only negative options. They approach the bottom of the whirlpool with no choice but continued destruction.

Alcoholism, for the alcoholic, is a *learned response* to living which is maladaptive. As the disease progresses, the alcoholic becomes increasingly maladaptive. He becomes less and less well equipped to employ options that work. Alcoholism, for the person involved with an alcoholic, is also a *learned response* to living which also becomes maladaptive. The more the spouse responds destructively, the more she is forced to. Both respond and rerespond with continued and ever increasing harmful actions. Most spouses of alcoholics enter marriages as healthy as other people. They cannot stay that way, however, by adjusting to their partner's alcoholism. *Adjusting to alcoholism is maladaptive. It doesn't work!*

Now for the good side. *If one partner makes a change, the other partner must accommodate to that change with changes of his own to balance the relationship, else it ceases to exist.* That's the nature of relationships. With help from outside the whirlpool, either partner can stop the destruction for himself. When he does, his partner is going to have to accommodate to that change to restore the balance of the relationship, or it will cease to exist. Either way, the partner reaching outside the whirlpool of alcoholism for help cannot lose. At the very least she stops her own destruction, at the most she makes it possible for her partner to stop his as well.

In alcoholic marriages it is only when one of the partners reaches for help that both can be helped. When one of the partners starts to replace negative actions with positive actions, the climate is set for constructive changes in the other partner. *Every positive change made by the partner reaching for help contains the potential for positive responses from the other.*

Had Ken sought help for himself, he could have recognized Barbara's failing performance and angry attacks as symptoms of alcoholism. Instead of feeling personally used and abused, he could have seen her need for treatment and, in her contrite moments, could have offered and insisted upon it. By responding positively to Barbara's harmful acts, Ken could have avoided pain for himself while providing the opportunity for Barbara to end her own destruction by accepting the treatment she so desperately needed.

Alcoholics will sometimes have their fill of destruction and will make the positive change of getting sober; then the nonalcoholic partner has to make changes, or the relationship will cease to exist. But it's risky business waiting for the alcoholic to have his fill. It's far better business for the alcoholic's partner to get help, for, not being addicted, the nonalcoholic can be reached earlier. Not being addicted, the nonalcoholic is more amenable to rational thinking and can see the whirlpool and the helping hand better than the alcoholic, who is in the throes of *chemical insanity*. For these reasons, I have addressed this book to you—spouse, partner, employer, friend, child or parent—rather than to the alcoholic.

By seeking knowledge about the disease and by restoring your own emotional security, you will be forcing the alcoholic into a position where demands for change are placed upon him. The chances are good that he too will recover. By seeking help you will also be able to bring new directions and meaning to your own life, regardless of how the alcoholic chooses to respond. That's guaranteed! If you do not choose to get help for yourself, you will be faced, after further pain, with desertion, divorce, or the premature death of your spouse. Aside from recovery, these are the only avenues out of alcoholism. There is help available to you, both nonprofessional and professional. You begin to redirect your life the moment you reach for help.

Alcoholics Anonymous, Al-Anon, and Alateen are nonprofessional organizations which help alcoholics and their families and friends. Alcoholics Anonymous is primarily for alcoholics, but many of its meetings are open to anyone interested or involved with the disease. Al-Anon is for the adult family members and friends of alcoholics, whether the alcoholics are drinking or not. Alateen is for the children, relatives or friends of alcoholics who are under twenty-one and over eleven. (Sometimes younger children attend Alateen and fit very nicely into the program.) All the meetings are free unless you care to chip in for the coffee, and none have any other requirements. You need not even give your name unless you choose to.

Alcoholics Anonymous is the largest, most successful self-help group the world has ever known. Forty years ago, one alcoholic who couldn't stay sober, named Bill W., met another Alcoholic, Dr. Bob, who couldn't get sober. Together they got and stayed sober, and then they told other alcoholics how they did it and invited them along. One by one other alcoholics joined them and they got and stayed sober too. History was made! For the first time alcoholics, once considered totally hopeless, were recovering in large numbers. They were even staying recovered and they were doing it with the help they received in Alcoholics Anonymous, the organization that came into being when those first two alcoholics were joined by a third.

Today AA is worldwide and totals over 800,000 members who have gained their sobriety and entrance back into the world by following the AA program. Alcoholics Anonymous is listed in the telephone directories of virtually every city and village throughout the United States and Canada. For those interested or involved in the disease, AA meetings are educational and offer a tremendous source of hope and inspiration. Living, laughing, friendly, grateful evidence that recovery is possible exists and is demonstrated at every open AA meeting.

But the primary source of nonprofessional help for adult family members or friends of alcoholics resides in the Al-Anon Family Group meetings. When that first alcoholic sobered up, his wife, Lois, met other wives and then other relatives and friends who were eager to help and eager to change. Thus Al-Anon came into being and has continued to grow until it too has spread around the world. Al-Anon is not as large an organization as AA, which it is modeled after but separate from, so it is not always available in every community. Still, in North America it is within the reach of most people and like AA is listed in the local telephone directories under Al-Anon Family Groups. If Al-Anon is not available in a particular area, open AA meetings provide an opportunity to meet other wives, husbands, and friends of alcoholics. It takes only two or three to form an Al-Anon group.

Alateen members meet to exchange experiences and to gain knowledge. Like their Al-Anon parent, teenagers benefit *beyond* an understanding of the disease and how to respond to it. They become enlightened about themselves and through Alateen they learn to guide their own lives more meaningfully. Like their Al-Anon parents, they find inspiration and strength in the group.

Al-Anon is a powerful self-help group that is very effective in helping its members gain an understanding of themselves as well as the disease. Al-Anon is well aware that it is the spouse's own actions and reactions that will make or break her. Thus, it emphasizes the necessity of meeting one's own needs through constructive actions, doing what is right for one's self, knowing that only then do others stand to profit. Al-Anon helps the spouses make the natural law of relationships work for instead of against them. It knows that when the spouse begins to make constructive changes in her own behavior, the alcoholic is then pressured to make changes in return, and that those changes are often constructive. Spouses can rest assured that they are no longer contributing to the progression of the disease. They also can enjoy, perhaps for the first time in years, a resurgence of their own self-esteem and productivity.

Spouses often change enormously, only to find that their alcoholics are still ensnared in active alcoholism. Al-Anon does not then necessarily assist the spouse in taking definitive action to intervene more actively in the alcoholic's disease because it does not direct itself to the treatment needs of the alcoholic. Often the spouse will feel a need for further guidance in instances where the alcoholic remains recalcitrant, feeling that there is more she could be doing now that she has regained her strength. She may encounter the attitude often expressed by members of AA and Al-Anon that "You can't help an alcoholic until he wants it," but she should proceed past that attitude, because more is known about alcoholism today.

The assumption that "You can't help an alcoholic until he wants it" is erroneous and *is not inherent* in the program or philosophy of AA on which Al-Anon is based. AA holds simply that AA cannot help the alcoholic until he wants help. AA *does not* say, "He can't be helped until he wants help" but *does* admit, "He can't be helped *by us* until he wants help."

There are millions of alcoholics in need of help. Less than 5 percent of them are in AA. Yet there is no other organization or treatment modality which even begins to approach the number AA reaches. Obviously there are a lot of alcoholics at large not wanting help. That does not mean they cannot be reached and helped. It does mean, however, that if left to their own devices, at least 95 percent of all alcoholics and their families are destined for continued destruction and the premature death of the alcoholic. We cannot afford to let this happen. Alcoholism is ever on the increase. This year there are an estimated 9 million alcoholics in the United States alone who directly affect more than 36 million family members, employers, and friends. Next year there will be more. Alcoholism is increasing rapidly. The annual cost to the nation's economy has been estimated at $15 billion. Approximately 55% of all traffic fatalities are related to alcohol abuse. The cost in human misery is beyond measure. We cannot afford to take a passive stand.

AA has a marvelous way of expanding as is needed and can easily accommodate itself to tremendous growth. AA cannot, however, go out and drag those millions of alcholics into its church basements, homes, club houses, and meeting halls. AA'ers are practical. They have learned to face reality. They know they do not have any leverage over the alcoholic who has not come to them for help. Only families and employers have that kind of leverage.

AA has as its First Step the alcoholic's admission of powerlessness over alcohol and the unmanageability of his life. With that admission, the alcoholic can then go on and get well with the rest of AA's program. Family members and employers make possible that admission when they stop the destructive actions of rewarding the alcoholic for drinking and start letting him suffer the consequences of his drinking. The alcoholic cannot make that admission—he cannot come to that awareness and acceptance of powerlessness and unmanageability—when families and employers help him to manage and to feel O.K. again after each drinking crisis. With so many people around picking up the pieces, the alcoholic cannot see his powerlessness or how unmanageable his life has become. AA can help the alcoholic, but only when families and employers stop helping him with his drinking. When they do, they make his recovery possible. If only by restraint, he is *forced* to face the reality of his condition.

We no longer need to be afraid of the words "force," "coercion," "leverage," "intervention," or "influence." Most alcoholics will not get well unless pressured to do so by others. Coercion, force, leverage, intervention, and influence are simply means by which the people around the alcoholic make it possible for him to "reach bottom," the prerequisite for recovery. Our knowledge of alcoholism has expanded enormously in recent years. Thanks to AA, which proved once and for all that alcoholism was treatable, the disease has been studied and researched, and our knowledge of it has expanded enormously in recent years. Although much is still not known, we do know today that alcoholics can be made to want help. They can be brought to an earlier recognition of their condition and their need to change than is possible if they are left alone.

Al-Anon does this indirectly but very effectively. By concentrating on the treatment of the family members, pressures to change are placed on the alcoholics by healthy actions of the family. And the climate for change is also provided as the family members refrain from actions which hurt the alcoholic by helping him to drink. Thousands of alcoholics are sober today simply because their families got well, thus forcing their alcoholics to an earlier bottom and treatment.

Thousands more are sober today because family members, particularly but not exclusively spouses, are directly intervening in the alcoholic's disease. Ronnie is typical of these spouses. She changed enormously through Al-Anon, but John continued to drink anyway. Ronnie knew the marriage could not go on much longer as it was, so she sought counseling. Al-Anon met her needs for gaining emotional health but could not help her meet John's special needs. With counseling she learned the dynamics and techniques of direct confrontation and received, as well, assistance and guidance specific to her needs. She and her children were then able to intervene effectively in John's disease.

Margaret, too, received counseling and says she could not have forced Gary to treatment without it. Margaret role-played with her counselor the interchange they both knew would take place at the airport. "My counselor played Gary and I played myself. I knew exactly where my weaknesses were before I met Gary and was able to deal with them. I also had come to the point in Al-Anon where I knew my strengths and that I could rely upon them."

Neither Ronnie nor Margaret felt that their counseling and their Al-Anon involvement conflicted with each other. Both felt a need to do more—if more was possible—for their recalcitrant husbands as their own health improved, although both admitted that when they first attended Al-Anon they didn't want to "waste time" on themselves and were concerned only that something should be done with their husbands. They soon recognized their own needs, however, and went about meeting them before attempting more than they could handle with their husbands' disease.

Margaret sought counseling soon after joining Al-Anon. Gary's drinking was such that he frequently presented situations that seemed to call for direct confrontations. Margaret wanted to intervene at these times but did not know what to do specifically and was aware that she might "botch it" without assistance. John was just always quietly drunk, or so it seemed to Ronnie. She didn't feel as if he presented crises she could get her hands on, yet she wanted to do something. With counseling and increased emotional security, she was able to use John's minor but frequent crises accumulatively in a direct confrontaion. Both Gary and John required more than health on the part of their spouses. Margaret and Ronnie received additional help and were thus able to meet their husbands' needs. Because they did Gary and John were able to begin their recoveries.

Some alcoholics do need more than others! The fact that they are not responding to what is being done does not mean there is nothing more to do. Yet one has to know how far one can go. No one can be asked to sacrifice himself to save the alcoholic. Ronnie had reached the point of knowing she was no longer willing to continue the marriage if John refused treatment. She wanted to do what she could but was prepared to move on in case she was not successful.

Most alcoholics are married and/or employed. Only families (or close friends) and employers can reach the 90 percent or more still untreated. Al-Anon is the largest and best resource available to family members. When family members are helped to change themselves, at least 50 percent of their alcoholics recover as well, and AA can grow to accommodate all those who wish to join its ranks. The emotional security achieved by the family members through Al-Anon may, as well, lead to more definitive action, which can then help even more alcoholics, who will also be cheerfully accommodated by AA if they so choose.

Professional counseling is available for the family member who needs more in the way of help either in gaining emotional security or in being more direct in the intervention process. Counseling can do some things that Al-Anon cannot do. Al-Anon is the best medium for reaching the millions of suffering people who are involved with an alcoholic, but it cannot meet all the needs of some of them. Both Al-Anon and professional counseling help family members in gaining an understanding of themselves and the disease. Both help family members to refrain from harmful actions and to take constructive action, and they help the family members to recognize and meet their own needs. When Al-Anon and counseling are combined, the process of recovery is probably faster. Professional counselors are more aware of the specific needs of both the spouse and the alcoholic. While helping the family member restore her emotional security, they can help her to take more definitive action with the alcoholic when and if she feels ready and if it is needed. But counseling alone can never provide the friendship, love, inspiration, and hope to be found in Al-Anon. Counseling services also can never, no matter how much they expand, be available for all the people suffering from their involvement with alcoholism. Al-Anon, which has the same ability to expand as has AA, can be available to all.

Alcoholics Anonymous and Al-Anon Family Groups are listed in local telephone directories. For further information write to AA World Services, Inc., P. O. Box 459, Grand Central Station, New York, New York 10017, and to Al-Anon Family Group Headquarters, P.O. Box 182, Madison Square Station, New York, New York 10010.

Sources of information about alcoholism counseling resources available in your community include:

1. Hospitals in your area. Telephone to find out which ones treat alcoholism and which ones have alcoholism counseling services.
2. National Council on Alcoholism local affiliate. If it is not listed in your telephone directory, write to the National Council on Alcoholism, 2 Park Avenue, New York, New York 10016.

Many local affiliates of the National Council maintain information centers where you can seek information or treatment facilities for yourself as well as the alcoholic. Often they have names of physicians knowledgeable about alcoholism as well as hospitals, clinics, rehabilitation centers, and counseling services.

3. Alcohol and Drug Problems Association of North America, 1130 Seventeenth Street, N.W., Washington, D.C. 20036. The association has a *Directory of Alcoholism Treatment Facilities* which lists more than 2,565 centers in the United States and Canada, some of which have counseling services for family members. Include the cost of $7.50 plus $.50 postage.

You do not have to wait to seek help. You do not need to know "for sure" that your spouse is an alcoholic. The time to go for help is when you have any questions at all about his drinking. That's what Sally did. She knew only that somehow Tom's drinking was interfering with her life. By seeking help early she was able to discover the true nature of the problem, and thus was able to respond to it constructively almost from the beginning. And Tom was forced very early in his disease to accept the help he needed.

Find out about the disease and whether alcoholism is in fact your problem. There is no harm in seeking information; rather, it is a sign of health. There is no such thing as a stupid question in either Al-Anon, AA or counseling. Keep going and keep asking until questions are answered to your satisfaction. Bear in mind that earlier detection will result in less destruction to you and yours. Bear in mind as well that the recovery rate is higher for alcoholics who are treated before they have lost their families and jobs.

The sooner you seek help, the sooner you can respond appropriately. Like Sally, you can learn early to use the natural law which exists in relationships by responding constructively, thereby enriching your own life while creating the potential for constructive changes in your partner, whether his alcoholism has been determined yet or not.

12

FREEDOM

Alcoholics are dependent people. They are psychologically and eventually physically dependent upon alcohol, and they are emotionally dependent upon people close to them. This is true in spite of the alcoholic's behavior, which frequently appears to be quite independent, especially when he blusters, berates, abuses, threatens, and leaves home for periods of time. Because of the alcoholic's dependent nature, spouses, parents, partners, children, and even siblings are in an important position to apply leverage in obtaining help for the alcoholic, even when he doesn't want it.

Alcoholics cannot stand alone. Out of their needs they grant power to the people closest to them. Therefore the meaningful people in the lives of alcoholics can either perpetuate the disease or initiate recovery.

It is not easy to be involved with an alcoholic. Perpetuating the disease spells destruction for all involved. Taking steps to initiate recovery is also painful for all involved, yet it is the only route which holds promise for something better, and it is a route made infinitely easier once the person involved with the alcoholic accepts the alcoholism as an established and undeniable fact. Only then is that person in a position to switch from abetting the progression of the disease to initiating the alcoholic's recovery. Acceptance frees you! It keeps you from misdirected action and wasted energy.

If you wish the alcoholic to recover, you have no real choice but to change your ways: you have no real choice but to start assuming attitudes and performing actions which hold promise and to stop the ones which guarantee disaster. You are no longer compelled to do all those things which you never wanted to do in the first place. Your alcoholic cannot force you to do them unless you allow him to. The choice is yours. No one can tell you what to do. You should be told, however, what *won't* work and what *might* work.

The following annotated prescription for recovery shows the usual actions of those involved with alcoholics, how these responses are destructive, and what can be done instead. Because the usual responses to alcoholism are so natural as to be universal, they are presented as assumed actions which you no longer have to do. Because the constructive responses to alcoholism are so rarely used, they are presented as new actions which should be *started*.

The new actions to be started are all constructive in nature; as such, they *guarantee* positive results. They will enable you to regain and maintain your own emotional health. They will keep you from being destroyed by the disease. They will allow you to bring new directions to your life which are in your best interests. They also offer the chance for initiating your alcoholic's recovery; and the chance is a good one, because each constructive response forces the alcoholic *on some level, to some degree,* to see the reality of his condition. Only then can he see his need to change.

You no longer have to run from the disease.
START learning the facts about alcoholism.

- Find out once and for all if alcoholism is the problem; if it is, give up and accept it. Only then will you be able to change the things that can be changed.
- As long as alcoholism is denied, it will progress and so will your suffering. Struggling against acceptance will cause your actions to be misdirected and your energies to be wasted.
- Start attending Al-Anon meetings and open AA meetings. Read the literature.
- Knowledge is power, you will need it.

You no longer have to blame the alcoholic.
START concentrating on your own actions—they are what will make or break you.

- Let go of what the alcoholic is doing. Stop blaming him for everything. It is your actions and reactions that will make or break you, not what the alcoholic does.
- Examine your feelings and actions. What are your means of coping? How well do you really feel about yourself? Would you like to feel better? Are your actions helping the alcoholic? Or are you helping to make his life more manageable? Are you letting him see that he is powerless over alcohol? While continuing at Al-Anon, seek professional counseling if you feel a need for more. Go to any lengths to gain the knowledge, insight, and strength necessary for you to cope with alcoholism in a manner healthy to you and to the alcoholic.

You no longer have to control the alcoholic's drinking.
START concentrating on his need for treatment and START offering treatment.

- Let him drink as much and as often as he pleases whenever he pleases. He's going to anyway! Any of your attempts to stop him or to control him will fail. You cannot afford to fail! Your attempts at control will grant him the "justification" he's looking for to continue drinking.
- Each time he drinks to excess, causing suffering to himself or others, indicates his need for treatment. Offer treatment at these times, but do it when he's sober. If he's drunk he will not listen. Offer treatment when he's hurting; do not offer treatment when he has himself all put together again. That's too late.
- Whenever he either agrees to treatment or asks for it, get him to it immediately. Given any time at all, he'll talk himself and you right out of it.
- Have AA phone numbers to call; have at hand numbers of alcoholism counseling services, alcoholism counselors, and physicians knowledgeable about alcoholism; and know of local hospitals that treat alcoholics. Get your alcoholic to the place and people that seem most appropriate to you at the time.

You no longer have to rescue the alcoholic.
START letting him suffer and assume responsibility for each and every consequence of his drinking.

- Every crisis caused by his drinking is an opportunity for him to receive the message from reality telling him, "Your drinking is out of control. Your life is unmanageable." He cannot get well until he receives that message. You intercept delivery of that message every time you rescue the alcoholic in *any* way. If you want him to get the message, stop intercepting it; stop rescuing!
- Whenever you bail him out of jail, call his boss with an excuse for his absence, make good his bad checks, tell lies to cover for him, locate his lost car, nurse his hangover, pick him up off the floor, or in any other way protect him from the consequences of his drinking, you are making his drinking more tolerable. You are mak-

ing his life more manageable. You are keeping him from knowing how bad it really is.

• Without messages from reality in the form of crises caused by his drinking, he cannot stop drinking; he won't be able to see that he has to.

• Let your attitude be, "You did it, you are responsible." Let your words tell that you are willing to get him to treatment, that his behavior indicates a need for treatment, a need he has to at least talk to someone about his drinking. Show your willingness to do anything to help him get well. Show your unwillingness to do anything to lighten his drinking burdens. After all, if he is willing to drink even though his drinking causes problems, then he should be willing to assume the responsibility for the consequences of those problems. Let him!

• The times it will be most difficult for you to refuse to rescue him will be when his earning powers are in any way threatened. You will urgently feel the need at these times to make excuses and to tell lies to cover him—to pull him out of "just this scrape"—so that his job will not be jeopardized. *DON'T.* If you do, you will only prolong his drinking and the job will be lost anyway. You might tell his employer the truth. Maybe he can help you get your alcoholic to treatment; many do.

You no longer have to be concerned with the alcoholic's reasons for drinking.
START resuming a normal living pattern.

• There aren't any! Reasons are only excuses for the alcoholic; he needs them to continue drinking. Everyone has problems, but not everyone uses alcohol as a means for coping with them. So stop living your life as if you were walking on eggs; stomp a little bit, enjoy yourself! Your alcoholic's going to drink no matter what you do. Your pussyfooting around does not reduce his reasons for drinking; and it hurts you. It makes you dependent upon him; it makes it easier for him to drink and to wield his power over you.

• Renew old friendships and begin new ones. The more you become a shadow of the sick alcoholic, the greater your destruction, and the easier it is for him to continue drinking. You have your own life to live and you must live it. If you refuse to, you are allowing your alcoholic to destroy you and himself. With your resumption of normal living patterns, your alcoholic will find further excuses for drinking. Remember that he is going to find them no matter what you do.

• *On some level* your rejoining the world will force the alcoholic to compare his sick behavior with the more normal behavior of others. *On some level* rejoining the world will represent to the alcoholic a loss of control over you. You are changing; he is forced to accommodate; *he may decide to get well.*

You no longer have to threaten.
START saying what you mean and doing what you say.

• Explore all your options, examine the consequences of any actions you might take, then make decisions and *put them into action.*
• Say what you mean and mean what you say, and *if you say it, do it.* Only then will the alcoholic begin to believe you. Only then will he begin to take you seriously, which he must do if you wish to be influential in getting him to treatment. Be believable; be serious. Don't announce any intention unless you are sure to put it into action. Anything else renders you unbelievable.
• Threats diminish you! Threats feed into the alcoholic's grandiosity and help to keep him from feeling his need to change.

You no longer have to accept or extract promises.
START rejecting them.

• It isn't fair to ask for promises. The alcoholic can't keep them. Broken promises heighten his sense of inadequacy and cause him to feel unworthy of help.
• He cannot consistently modify his drinking, so he is neither believable nor trustworthy and won't be until he is treated. Why pretend otherwise? By asking for or accepting promises, you are telling your alcoholic you think he can control his drinking. He can't! If you pretend otherwise, he will not see his powerlessness.
• Refuse to accept his promises. By not accepting and by not asking for promises from your alcoholic you are giving him a very important message. *You are telling him he is too sick for that.*

You no longer have to seek advice from the uninformed.
START your commitment to treatment and long-range goals of health.

• If family, friends, clergy, and professionals do not have knowledge specific to the disease—and they won't have without specialized education—they will not be able to help you and they may hurt. Families and friends will have only "home remedies" to offer; "home remedies" are no more effective for alcoholism than they are for cancer or any other serious disease. Consequently trying them will only increase your sense of failure. The exhortations for greater demonstrations of will power so often delivered by uninformed clergymen and physicians do not speak to the disease; consequently they too increase everyone's sense of failure. Uninformed doctors also often prescribe sedatives and minor tranquilizers which serve only to prolong the progression of the disease while providing another chemical and the opportunity for a dual addiction.
• Adhere to your program of recovery even when it's painful! Stop looking for the easy ways out so often suggested by the uninformed. Continue your attendance

at Al-Anon. If Al-Anon is not available, attend open
AA meetings. Seek help from professionals in the field
of alcoholism—professional alcoholism counselors, or
social workers, clergymen, nurses, physicians, or psy-
chologists who have received specialized education and
training in the treatment of alcoholism. Go to any
lengths to secure the help you need.

*You no longer have to hide the fact that you are
seeking help.*
START telling the alcoholic that you are.

• Alcoholism is not a moral issue. It's a disease! Go
for treatment and keep going when he tries to stop you.
Your seeking treatment will represent to him a loss of
his control over you and he will feel threatened. He will
ridicule you, or threaten you, or plead with you or com-
plain about you. He will do anything to make you stop
seeking help. Don't stop!
• Your getting help shows your alcoholic that you care
for him, that there is help available, that he is worthy of
help and can be helped.
• Your going for help means you are serious and he
knows it. His drinking won't be quite the same any
more. It may seem to get worse for a while, but for
sure, it won't be as much fun; you are ruining it!

You no longer have to nag, preach, coax, and lecture.
START reporting his inappropriate actions to him.

• He can't be coaxed or nagged out of a drink and he's
beyond your lectures and sermons! There are no exhortations strong enough to counteract his craving for his
fix, alcohol. Exhortations will serve only to make the
alcoholic feel more defensive and inadequate. To be receptive to treatment, he must feel less defensive, not
more so, and he must feel worthy of help.
• Look at his behavior: don't minimize it to yourself or

to your alcoholic. Facts are facts! Report the facts of the alcoholic's behavior—his actions—to him the next day when he's sober, then drop the subject to avoid nagging. But keep the pressure on; the next day review the new actions, then drop the subject again, and so on. Remember that he was anesthetized the night before and may not remember much of his behavior. Your reports will refresh his memory. Report his actions matter-of-factly. Express your concern for him and point out that his actions indicate a need for treatment, a need for seeking outside assistance. As you report his behavior, he will put the blame elsewhere. Don't let him! Bring it back to him by maintaining the attitude and the words that no matter what anyone else did or did not do, it is his actions that are under discussion. *Nothing is as important as how he reacts to it.*

• Don't get into any discussions with the alcoholic about whether he is an alcoholic or not. The point is, there are problems associated with his drinking that warrant outside help. Offer him the opportunity to see someone about the problems so that solutions can be investigated. If he refuses, end the discussion. It can be reopened next time.

You no longer have to allow the alcoholic to assault you or your children.
START protecting yourself.

• Do not let him assault you. He does not have that right. Don't give it to him.
• Call the police if necessary. Get an Order of Protection if necessary. Have him jailed if necessary. Leave him if necessary. Physical abuse destroys you both. Go to *any* lengths to avoid it.

You no longer have to be a puppet.
START detaching yourself.

• Stop jumping every time he pulls a string. No matter what strings he pulls. When you act like his puppet, you give him control and make him feel as if he's O.K. He's not O.K. He's dying. He can't see that he's sick if you act as if he's well!

• By responding to his demands, threats, pleadings, anger—any of his manipulations—with either acquiescence or emotional outbursts, you allow him to make you do things you don't want to do. Besides weakening your own sense of self-worth, you put him in the position of puppeteer. You make him your manager. He can't get well until he sees that he can't even manage himself, which he won't be able to see as long as he can manage you.

• Your alcoholic is an expert at pushing your buttons. He actually needs you to blow up and to be fearful of him or for him. He goes out of his way to get you to lose your cool. If you blow up, he has his justification for drinking. If you acquiesce, he is rescued once again from facing his behavior and its consequences. He wins another round in his fight to continue his destruction.

• If you concentrate on what is right for you, and therefore for him, by taking constructive action with the help and knowledge you are receiving, he no longer controls you. If you detach yourself from his sick or destructive behavior, you gain your freedom.

• You then change enormously. The alcoholic is forced to respond to your healthy changes with changes of his own. The odds are he'll choose sobriety—health for himself.

It is never too late to stop the old and start the new. The time to start is *now*. Perhaps the hardest part of stopping the old ways and beginning new ones is the underlying fear that the alcoholic won't be able to "make it" unless you do the very things you're supposed to be stopping.

To rid yourself of this fear, take a good look at the track record in terms of how well the alcoholic is actually "making it" today. Is it better now than two years ago, or five? Is he "making it" better now than then? You will probably discover that your helping has not interfered one iota with the destructive progression of his disease. With a closer look you will see that your helping only made it easier for him to continue drinking.

It is important also to review the record in terms of your own feelings, for you won't be able to make a change unless you believe it's right. Examine the responses you have been using, bearing in mind that it is your actions which will make or break you. How have they made you feel about yourself? Have they increased or decreased your sense of your own worth?

Do you feel shame, humiliation, fear, degradation, anger, resentment? Are you anxious? Do you feel sorry for yourself? Are your actions bringing you peace of mind, confidence, hope? Or is everything going from bad to worse?

Naturally, if your ways are working there is no need for change. It is only when you perceive that your ways are not working that you will see the need. And at that point any change will seem right, even if only because it's a change.

You may feel it isn't fair that you have to change; after all, he's the alcoholic! If he hadn't become an alcoholic, none of this would have happened and such incredible demands would not have been placed upon you. That may be true. Then again, something worse might have happened instead. Life is not fair. Your alcoholic doesn't think it's fair either. He would have chosen otherwise had he been able.

To respond effectively to your alcoholic, you will have to act in ways which seem unnatural and which will therefore be uncomfortable for you. The new acts will seem strange; some you've never been taught, and some you've been taught to avoid. But don't let that stop you. Alcoholism is an unnatural condition; the ways out of it are also unnatural. As you begin to act differently, you will start feeling differently. Pretty soon you will wonder how you ever lived the way you did.

Be prepared for flak from your alcoholic as you begin doing new things, acting in new ways. He will want you the way you were and will be very resistant to your changes. He will feel threatened because he knows that if you maintain your changes, he's going to have to change as well, and he does not want to change. He may very well muster up all his energies to subvert and thwart you any way he can. Hang tight! Have the faith that you can't lose by doing what you now know is right. You can only win.

Responding constructively to your partner's alcoholism will require the greatest effort you have ever put into anything in your life. And it's a daily effort, not a one-shot deal. It's the long haul you will be going for that will require you to break your life into manageable sections—days! Every day, for the day, with persistence and determination, concentrate on only those acts which you know have a chance. Let go of how your alcoholic responds. You will be able to measure the effects of your new actions only in retrospect, after you've been performing them for several months. It will not be the actions of one day your alcoholic will respond to, it will be your daily actions accumulated over a period of time, which you can best perform by concentrating only on what you have to do today—letting go of yesterday, putting aside tomorrow. A daily check list of actions that are effective in responding to alcoholism are provided at the end of this chapter. If you perform these actions, one day at a time, you guarantee your recovery, and very likely your alcoholic's.

It's all up to you. Your actions can either cause you to grow, bringing a resurgence of your energy, self-confidence, and peace of mind, or they can cause you to suffer further. Your actions as well can either perpetuate your alcoholic's disease or make possible his recovery.

Combating alcoholism and its destruction requires

your greatest efforts. It can also bring you the greatest rewards you've ever known. Alcoholics can get "weller than well" and so can their spouses. You can come to act in ways you've never acted; you can come to feel in ways you've never felt. You can become beautiful and free!

GUARANTEED Rx FOR RECOVERY

- You no longer have to run from the disease.
  Start learning the facts about alcoholism.

- You no longer have to blame the alcoholic.
  Start concentrating on your own actions—they are what will make or break you.

- You no longer have to control the alcoholic's drinking.
  Start concentrating on his need for treatment and *start* offering treatment.

- You no longer have to rescue the alcoholic.
  Start letting him suffer and assume responsibility for each and every consequence of his drinking.

- You no longer have to be concerned with the alcoholic's reasons for drinking.
  Start resuming a normal living pattern.

- You no longer have to threaten.
  Start saying what you mean and doing what you say.

- You no longer have to accept or extract promises.
  Start rejecting them.

- You no longer have to seek advice from the uninformed.

Start your commitment to treatment and long-range goals of health.

- You no longer have to hide the fact that you are seeking help.
  Start telling the alcoholic that you are.

- You no longer have to nag, preach, coax, and lecture.
  Start reporting his inappropriate actions to him.

- You no longer have to allow the alcoholic to assault you or your children.
  Start protecting yourself.

- You no longer have to be a puppet.
  Start detaching yourself.

NEW FROM BALLANTINE!

FALCONER, John Cheever   27300 $2.25

The unforgettable story of a substantial, middle-class man and the passions that propel him into murder, prison, and an undreamed-of liberation. "CHEEVER'S TRIUMPH . . . A GREAT AMERICAN NOVEL."—*Newsweek*

GOODBYE, W. H. Manville   27118 $2.25

What happens when a woman turns a sexual fantasy into a fatal reality? The erotic thriller of the year! "Powerful."—*Village Voice*. "Hypnotic."—*Cosmopolitan*.

**THE CAMERA NEVER BLINKS, Dan Rather
with Mickey Herskowitz**   27423 $2.25

In this candid book, the co-editor of "60 Minutes" sketches vivid portraits of numerous personalities including JFK, LBJ and Nixon, and discusses his famous colleagues.

THE DRAGONS OF EDEN, Carl Sagan 26031 $2.25

An exciting and witty exploration of mankind's intelligence from pre-recorded time to the fantasy of a future race, by America's most appealing scientific spokesman.

VALENTINA, Fern Michaels   26011 $1.95

Sold into slavery in the Third Crusade, Valentina becomes a queen, only to find herself a slave to love.

**THE BLACK DEATH, Gwyneth Cravens
and John S. Marr**   27155 $2.50

A totally plausible novel of the panic that strikes when the bubonic plague devastates New York.

**THE FLOWER OF THE STORM,
Beatrice Coogan**   27368 $2.50

Love, pride and high drama set against the turbulent background of 19th century Ireland as a beautiful young woman fights for her inheritance and the man she loves.

**THE JUDGMENT OF DEKE HUNTER,
George V. Higgins**   25862 $1.95

Tough, dirty, shrewd, telling! "The best novel Higgins has written. Deke Hunter should have as many friends as Eddie Coyle."—*Kirkus Reviews*

LG-2

Learn to live with somebody... *yourself.*